STUDENT WORKBOOK

FOR

WRITING AND REPORTING NEWS

A COACHING METHOD

MEDIA ENHANCED FOURTH EDITION

STUDENT WORKBOOK

FOR

WRITING AND REPORTING NEWS

A COACHING METHOD

MEDIA ENHANCED FOURTH EDITION

Carole Rich
Hofstra University, New York

THOMSON

WADSWORTH

Australia • Canada • Mexico • Singapore • Spain • United Kingdom • United States

Printed in the United States of America [or Canada]
1   2   3   4   5   6   7   07   06   05   04

Printer: Patterson Printing Company

0-534-63337-4

For more information about our products, contact us at:
Thomson Learning Academic Resource Center
1-800-423-0563

For permission to use material from this text or product, submit a request online at
http://www.thomsonrights.com
Any additional questions about permissions can be submitted at
thomsonrights@thomson.com

Thomson Wadsworth
10 Davis Drive
Belmont, CA 94002-3098
USA

Asia
Thomson Learning
5 Shenton Way #01-01
UIC Building
Singapore 068808

Australia/New Zealand
Thomson Learning
102 Dodds Street
Southbank, Victoria 3006
Australia

Canada
Nelson
1120 Birchmount Road
Toronto, Ontario M1K 5G4
Canada

Europe/Middle East/South Africa
Thomson Learning
High Holborn House
50/51 Bedford Row
London WC1R 4LR
United Kingdom

Latin America
Thomson Learning
Seneca, 53
Colonia Polanco
11560 Mexico D.F.
Mexico

Spain/Portugal
Paraninfo
Calle/Magallanes, 25
28015 Madrid, Spain

Contents

STUDENT WORKBOOK

FOR

WRITING AND REPORTING NEWS

A COACHING METHOD

MEDIA ENHANCED FOURTH EDITION

Write From the Start: A Coaching Method

1

The following exercises are designed to help you start writing news stories. These exercises will help you identify the focus of a story and consider the importance of graphics. Use the tell-a-friend technique explained in Chapter 1 to write your story in a clear, conversational manner.

1-1. Crime story

Read the following information and write a focus sentence at the top of your story. Then jot down an order for your story. Assume that you are a reporter in Tampa, Fla., and you are writing this story for the Monday morning newspaper.

Location: Riverview section of Tampa.

Facts: This information comes from Tampa sheriff's deputies: Two robbers burst into a home in Riverview at 11:30 p.m. Sunday. The home was owned by Grace Ford, 20. Ford was sitting in a front room with her baby, Brandi, 10 months old, who was in a playpen. Ford's sister, Cynthia, 16, also was in the room.

According to sheriff's reports: Both men were described as white, from 18 to 20 years old and of medium height and weight. One man was wearing a ski mask and jogging pants with the letters "UF" (for University of Florida) on the side. The other wore a white shirt and a baseball cap. Neighbors heard shots and called the sheriff's deputies. The men got away in a car that had been waiting in a nearby cemetery.

[This information comes from an interview with Grace Ford.]

She said the robbers pushed her, her baby and her sister from room to room. They took about $5,000 worth of jewelry. The dog, a Rottweiler named Elka, began barking. The robbers fired three shots at the dog. They missed. The baby began crying. Ford said she picked her up and found a bullet hole in Brandi's diaper with the bullet imbedded in the diaper. Direct quotes from Ford: "There was about an inch left to the diaper that it didn't pierce. They were extra thick."

Based on a story from the *St. Petersburg* (Fla.)*Times.* Used with permission.

1-2. Find the focus

Read the following information and ask yourself what is the most important or interesting fact. Write a focus sentence identifying that newsworthy angle:

a. The New England Journal of Medicine released a study today. The study says people who abruptly quit drinking coffee may suffer effects of caffeine withdrawal. Some of the symptoms include headaches, depression, anxiety and fatigue. The study says that even people who drink fewer than three cups of coffee a day may be affected.

b. A new law went into effect yesterday in Maine. The law affects all businesses that have more than 15 employees. The law requires employers to educate workers about sexual harassment. Under the law, employers must post notices explaining that sexual harassment is illegal and must notify workers about how they may file a complaint with the Maine Human Rights Commission.

c. A band is scheduled to perform on your campus this weekend. The band is named Elvis Hitler. The band was booked by John Musiclover, a senior who heads a group that promotes cultural diversity on campus. Musiclover says the band is not a racist group. But several students on campus claim the name of the band is offensive, and they want the performance to be canceled.

d. Police suspected two men of drug dealing. Police witnessed the men exchanging money and what appeared to be heroin. But after they arrested the men, police couldn't find the heroin. Police called in their drug-sniffing dog. The dog headed directly to one man's sneakers. Inside the sneakers was a pound of heroin. The two men were charged with drug trafficking.

e. A man in your community received a postcard yesterday from his father, who lived in a nearby town and had just returned from a trip. "Please come over so your mother and I can show you pictures of our trip," the postcard said. "I guess my father wondered why I never came over," said the son, Jason Gott. His father and mother died several years ago. The postcard that arrived yesterday was sent 30 years ago.

1-3. Online focus: headlines and blurbs

Write an online headline and summary blurb for each of the previous focus sentences that you wrote. Try to limit your headlines to six words and your summary blurbs to one or two sentences. Your focus sentence may serve as your summary blurb if you wrote it well.

1-4. Visual elements

a. Write a facts box for the following information:

The health center at your university has issued a press release about preventing frostbite in winter climates, especially for skiers. Mike Chapman, a physical therapist at the center, said students should not drink alcohol before they head outdoors. He said alcohol dehydrates the body and makes people more susceptible to frostbite. Some of the signs of frostbite include: extreme pain, numbness, white or whitish-blue or whitish-yellow areas, blisters and black coloration of the affected areas. If you suspect you have frostbite, follow these tips: Do not rub the affected areas. Re-warm the area with warm, not hot, water. If normal color does not return within 20 minutes, consult a physician.

b. Write an empowerment box for the following information:

The voter registration deadline for residents in your community is Oct. 19 for the Nov. 3 general election. The county clerk's office where people can register will be open from 8 a.m. to 9 p.m. starting Tuesday through Oct. 19. People who plan to be out of the county on Election Day can receive an absentee ballot. These voters must complete an affidavit at the clerk's office. They can cast the ballot there or take it with them. The absentee ballot must be received by noon, Nov. 2, and must be returned by 7 p.m., Nov. 3. People who are physically sick or disabled also may apply for absentee ballots. Residents may register to vote at any one of these sites: the county clerk's office at 11th and Main streets; the Democratic Party headquarters at 900 Main Street; the county public library at 300 Literary Drive.

c. Write a pull quote based on the following information:

The Women's Student Union sponsored a rally last night on your campus to celebrate Women's Equality Day. Connie Stauffer, president of the group, made the following comments: "I think we need to make sure that candidates for the upcoming election have a platform that includes women's rights. We need to make sure that government is held accountable. Our problems have not been addressed by our representatives in Congress. It makes me sick in my heart to think we are still fighting for things we were fighting for 20 years ago. It's time for a change."
Based on a story from *The University Daily Kansan.* Used with permission.

1-5. Style quiz

The following sentences are based on information in the previous stories. Correct the errors using Associated Press style. The most common errors in these sentences involve age, numbers, money, and time. Some of the sentences contain more than one error. Cross out the errors and write your corrections above them.

1. A diaper saved a 10 month old baby from a gunshot wound.

2. Grace Ford, a twenty year old mother, said the robbers stole 5000 dollars.

3. 10-month-old Brandi Ford was wearing an extra-thick diaper, which may have saved her life.

4. Grace Ford was sitting in her living room at 11:30 P.M. Sunday night when robbers burst into her home.

5. The ten-month-old baby was not harmed.

6. Right-handed females tend to live 5 years longer than left-handed females. Right-handed males lived ten years longer than left-handed males.

7. Residents may register to vote at the county clerk's office on Tuesday from 8 in the morning to 9 at night.

8. Jason Gott received a postcard thirty years late.

9. Even people who drink fewer than 3 cups of coffee a day may suffer caffeine withdrawal if they abruptly quit drinking coffee.

10. Businesses in Maine that have more than fifteen employees must educate workers about sexual harassment.

Changing Concepts of News 2

Some of the basic qualities in news stories involve conflict, timeliness, proximity, unusual nature, human interest and news about celebrities. Those concepts are still the same in online publications, but other concepts of news are changing. These exercises are intended to help you understand some of the basic qualities of news and the changing values of news. You may link directly to the Web sites mentioned in this chapter by accessing the site for this book at: *http://info.wadsworth.com/rich*.

2-1. Online news qualities

If you have access to the Internet, check online news sites in your state and discuss how they differ or are the same from print publications.

• To find a listing of online newspapers, type the Internet address for the Newslink site: *www.newslink.org*. Click on newspapers "By State" to find online newspapers in your state.

• If your local paper is online, compare the online version to the print version. What qualities of the online version differ from the print one? Are there any qualities of the site that would entice you to read the news online instead of in print?

• Access CNN at *www.cnn.com* and *www.msnbc.com*. List qualities of these sites that are unique to online publications such as interactivity and others.

• Discuss or list at least three features that you think an online site should contain.

• Discuss advantages and disadvantages of online news delivery. Explain why you would or would not want to receive your news online.

2-2. Convergent media

Working in small groups, discuss pros and cons of convergent media and partnerships between print and broadcast media. How will this trend affect the education of journalism students? List three advantages and three disadvantages of convergence in media organizations.

Advantages:

a. _____

b. _____

c. _____

Disadvantages

d. _____

e. _____

f. _____

2-3. Public (civic) journalism

Public journalism, also called "civic journalism," seeks to involve the community in issues. News organizations practicing this form of journalism often frame stories and projects by asking the community what issues they want explored. Critics of this type of coverage claim the news organizations lose their objectivity by getting involved in the stories and assuming an advocacy role.

• Check the Pew Center for Civic Journalism *www.pewcenter.org*. Discuss an issue in your community that might lend itself to civic journalism. Discuss the pros and cons of this form of journalism.

2-4. Qualities of news

Some of the main qualities of newsworthiness are timeliness, proximity (news in or near your community), unusual nature, prominence (stories about celebrities or prominent people), human interest and conflict. Some other newsworthy angles include entertainment, helpfulness (such as consumer news), trends (stories that show patterns in society). Using these qualities as your guide, identify the newsworthy elements in the following items; some items may have several qualities:

a. News qualities: _____

Ninety-eight alligators were found in the bedroom of a man who lives in Omaha, Neb.

b. News qualities: _____

The police department on your campus yesterday released crime statistics for the first six months of the semester.

c. News qualities: _____

A study released yesterday says that women who smoke at least a pack of cigarettes a day are more likely to have children with behavior problems than children of non-smokers.

d. News qualities: _____

Residents in your community are protesting plans by a developer to build a landfill on the outskirts of town.   They will express their feelings at a public hearing tonight.

e. News qualities: _____

Oprah Winfrey was named one of the richest women in America in the annual Forbes magazine ratings. Her production company generates about 40 percent of its revenue from the talk show.

f. News qualities: _____

A man in your town was gardening, but he didn't dig up weeds. He dug up his gold wedding band that he had lost 30 years ago.

g. News qualities: _____

The average age of college students is increasing. One out of four college students is over age 30.

2-5. Hard-news and feature stories

a. Using your community or campus newspaper, identify three hard-news stories and three feature stories.

b. Compare the qualities of news in the hard-news stories and the features. How do they differ?

The Basic News Story **3**

The following exercises will give you practice writing basic news stories. Write a focus sentence on top of your story as a guide for yourself. If you want a hard-news lead, your focus sentence could be the lead. If you want a creative lead, your focus sentence should be your nut graph. Before you begin writing, consider the order of the information you will use. Then write your story using the tell-a-friend technique. Place the most important facts high in the story.

3-1. Fire

Write a news story based on the following information. Decide what material needs to be attributed. Use yesterday as your time frame, but write the day of the week, which is the preferred AP style. Use a new paragraph for each new thought and a new paragraph for the start of a quotation.

This information comes from Lynn Wilbur, University Place assistant fire chief:
A fire occurred in a Tacoma suburb called University Place in Washington. Wilbur said the fire started in a corner unit at the Meadow Park Garden Court apartments. It spread to a two-bedroom apartment next door through a common attic the two apartments shared. Both apartment units were destroyed, and two others were damaged. Four families were left homeless. About 12 people had to be relocated. It was a two-alarm fire (which means two fire companies responded to the fire). Investigators have not confirmed the cause of the fire. The fire may have been started by a stove that was left on in one unit. "The pots were melted down on it." No one was injured. A pet cat died in the fire.

Information from apartment manager Steve Edwards:
He said he couldn't relocate the families in the apartment complex because it was filled to capacity. He said some residents may have to seek shelter with the American Red Cross.

Information from Rosemary Hurlburt, who lived in one of the apartments: Her apartment was gutted. She said she and her two daughters were at a convenience store when the fire started. She said she lost a lot of new possessions. "We just got new stuff," Hurlburt said. "My 5-year-old daughter just had a birthday party. We just got her a brand-new bunk bed set."

Based on a story from *The Oregonian.* Used with permission.

3-2. Program advance

A program about date rape will be offered at your school tonight. Your editor hands you a press release and tells you to write a story about the upcoming program. This type of story is called an advance. You interview one of the panelists who will be on the program and you get comments from people sponsoring the event. Instead of writing a lead announcing the program, try writing a lead based on something one of your sources tells you. Ask yourself what you find most important or interesting, and use that in your lead. Then write a nut graph giving the basic information about what, where, when and so forth. You do not need to use all the quotes. Here are your notes:

Notes from a press release: There will be a forum tonight about date rape. The program is called "Date Rape, Acquaintance Rape." It is sponsored by the Emily Taylor Women's Resource Center. The program will be held in the Pine Room of the Student Union on your campus. It will be conducted from 7 p.m. to 9 p.m. It is open to men and women. The forum will feature a film, "Campus Rape." Panelists will discuss issues in the film and an audience-participation discussion will follow.

Notes from interview with Sherill Robinson, graduate assistant in the Resource Center: She said the forum would address problems that contribute to date rape, such as miscommunication, drugs and alcohol. "Regardless of those things, unless a woman says 'yes,' it's rape," she said. She said she hoped people would become aware of what date rape was. She shows you an advertisement for the forum that defines date rape as forced sexual intercourse by someone you know.

Notes from interview with Barbara Ballard, director of the Resource Center: She said the center sponsored an outreach program, which brought sexual assault programs to residence halls, scholarship halls and fraternities. "When I came here there was no such thing as date rape or acquaintance rape," she said. "Those things didn't even have a title. Now it's a topic that's discussed, and people are a lot more educated about it."

Notes from interview with Sharon Danoff-Berg, a graduate assistant in the Emily Taylor Resource Center: At least one in four women will be sexually assaulted in their lifetime. About 90 percent of college rape victims are violated by someone they know. She says that is why she agreed to be one of four student panelists on the program. "There's this myth that most rapes are stranger rapes, where someone attacks you from out of the dark. That does happen, but not in the majority of rapes. People need to understand it's not the fault of the woman. Nobody deserves to be sexually assaulted or does anything to ask for it. The rapist is the one who needs to be held accountable."

Based on a story from *The University Daily Kansan.* Used with permission.

3-3. Online version

If you were writing the previous news story about date rape for the Web, what links and other information would you include? Search the Web for links and information about date rape.

3-4. Burglary

Write a news story based on the following information. Write a focus sentence on top of the story. You are a reporter for a Louisville newspaper, and you interviewed this man after you read the report of the burglary in the police records. Be careful to attribute any material that you cannot substantiate as factual. You do not have to use the quotes in one block. Use them where you think they fit best. Your time frame is yesterday (but use the day of the week).

Information from Louisville police Sgt. Frank Lavender: No one has been arrested. The item that was stolen has not been found. He said that this misfortune reinforces a point that police have been trying to convey to citizens: It's not enough just to lock your car. "We're trying to encourage people to look into their cars and see what's in there and put it in the trunk. People need to be more careful."

Information comes from Roy L. Jones, 60: He was having lunch with a friend at a Shoney's restaurant, 811 Eastern Parkway in Louisville. He parked his 1990 Oldsmobile in the restaurant parking lot. Inside the car he had a package wrapped in a plastic bag on the floor. When he returned to his car about 30 minutes after he entered the restaurant, the package was gone. The back door was open, and the glove compartment had been rifled. Inside the package was an $8,000 artificial leg. He had gone to Falls City Limb and Brace Co. before lunch to have his hip-to-floor prosthesis adjusted. He reported it to the police yesterday, but the leg has not turned up. He had locked the car, but the thief broke into it.

"I'm disgusted as hell, is all I can say. I bet whoever took it, when they opened the package is as disappointed as I am. I just hate to go through all the hassle of getting another one made. You have to go down there for a fitting, then you have to go down there again."

He said the leg is probably covered by insurance but that doesn't make him feel any better. He lost his left leg more than 30 years ago in an industrial accident. He uses a wheelchair when he goes out. He uses the artificial leg to move around his house. He had another one, but it no longer fit. He needed further amputation two years ago. That's why he needed the new leg. He lives at 950 Samuel St. in Germantown.
Based on a story from the (Louisville, Ky.) *Courier-Journal.* Used with permission.

3-5. Telephone bill

You are a reporter for your local newspaper, and your editor asks you to interview this man who has an unusual story. You call him, and he gives you this information. Write a focus statement on top of your story, and organize the material by the tell-a-friend method, placing the most interesting information high in the story. You can substitute your city or town for the town in this story or assume that you are a reporter for a wire service.

The man's name is Jim Tyler. He says he received a monthly telephone bill for July that amounted to $110,099.44. The bill said there would be a late penalty of $1,650.27 if payment were not received by Sept. 2. The bill was from Southwestern Bell Telephone. Tyler lives in Herington, Kansas. The calls of the longest durations were from Boston to China. One call lasted seven hours. It began at 10:36 p.m. on July 26. The charge for it was $690.

The majority of the calls originated from coin-operated phones in the Boston area. Calls had been placed to 53 foreign countries and to several locations in the United States, primarily along the East Coast. The bill is about a thousand times higher than his normal bill. It was 386 pages, 1 3/4 inches thick and required postage of $2.90. The bill listed 3,261 calls. Only 44 of them were made by Tyler.

The operator assured Tyler that he would not have to pay for calls to foreign countries or places in the United States that he had not called. Tyler thinks the problem resulted from someone illegally using his telephone credit card number. He says it is possible that his credit card number was stolen when his daughter, Trisa, used it to call home from a coin-operated phone in a Pittsburgh airport. She was returning from a church group trip to Kentucky when she tried to call home, but there was no answer.

Tyler says someone at the airport apparently saw her punch in his credit card number. He says the number may have been sold several times since then. He says he doesn't know how much of the bill he actually owes for his own calls. He thought something was strange when he received a call at 2 a.m. on July 27 from an operator asking him if he would authorize a credit card call to China. "I said, 'No, I don't even know anyone in a foreign country.' " He says the operator informed him that several calls to foreign countries had been made using his credit card number during the past several hours and that he could expect an astronomical phone bill. "By astronomical, I thought maybe $2,000 or $3,000."

Tyler is an administrator at the Lutheran Home care center in Herington. This telephone bill was for his home.

Based on a story from *The Topeka* (Kan.) *Capital-Journal.* Used with permission.

3-6. Quotes

This exercise is designed to help you decide what information should be in direct quotes and what should be paraphrased or not attributed at all. Edit this story by crossing out quotes where they don't belong or adding them where they do.

Package Arrives -- 25 Years Late

WASHINGTON (AP) -- A package from New York City to a Washington address finally arrived – albeit more than 25 years late.

"The package containing three 16 mm reels of the 1954 movie classic, 'On the Waterfront,' that was mailed July 3, 1974, was delivered Saturday to a townhouse in Northwest Washington," authorities said.

"The addressee, Martin Brinker of the District Living Cooperative, no longer lives there."

The package was left with Jason Ferguson, a 22-year-old George Washington University student.

"I'm going to grow up and graduate from college in less time than it took the U.S. Postal Service to deliver this," Ferguson said. "I would really like to think it's a hoax, but it doesn't look that way."

Postal Service spokesman Gus Ruiz said while things like this occur, they don't happen very often. "When they do, we have the same question, 'Where was it?' " he said.

Ruiz speculated because the films were shipped parcel post, they could have "been lost" either on a train or a bus.

"The package could have been stored in a holding area until their discovery," he said.

The films were sent insured by the Audio Film Center of Mount Vernon, N.Y.
Brinker apparently rented the film for $24 and the invoice warned him to "return promptly after use to avoid overtime charges.

Adapted from a story by The Associated Press. Used with permission.

3-7. Punctuating quotations

Edit this story for punctuation of quotations and attribution. Some sentences may contain too much or too little attribution.

A bar is an unlikely place to meet someone you will marry according to a researcher at the University of Chicago.

Philip Schumm, one of the researchers of a sex study, said "No more than 4 percent of dates that begin at a bar end up in marriage."

"The most common way of meeting a partner is the most ordinary way," said Schumm, a research associate at the University of Chicago. "Someone you know introduces you to someone they think you would like". he said. "That's the best way to meet someone," Schumm said.

Schumm and other Chicago social scientists wrote a book, "The Social Organization of Sexuality", which says that Americans are more conservative about sex than previous studies showed.

Early sex leads to failed relationships the researchers said. Only 2 percent of couples who had sex in the first two days of their relationship ended up getting married, the researchers said.

"I guess you could say this sheds some light on the limits of the casual pickup", Schumm said.

Adapted from a story by the McClatchy News Service.

3-8. Style quiz

This quiz will test your knowledge of Associated Press style for ages, percentages, addresses, money, numbers, titles, time and geographical regions. Some sentences contain more than one error. Cross out the errors and write your corrections above them.

1. The police officer in charge of the investigation was Sergeant Frank Lavender. *[handwritten: SGT.]*

2. The woman's daughter was just five years old. *[handwritten: 5]*

3. Fire officials said that twelve people had to be relocated because of the fire. *[handwritten: 12]*

4. The survey showed that ninety % of the American people lie routinely. *[handwritten: 90 percent]*

5. The artificial leg cost the man 8,000 dollars. *[handwritten: $]*

6. The 60 year old man lives at 950 Samuel Street in Louisville. *[handwritten: St.]*

7. Jim Tyler's phone bill last month was 110 thousand, ninety nine dollars and 44 cents. *[handwritten: $110,099.44]*

8. Most of the telephone calls were to places along the east coast of the U.S. *[handwritten: East Coast / United States]*

9. Tyler said 3261 calls were on the bill, which required postage of two dollars and ninety cents. *[handwritten: $2.90]*

10. One of the calls was placed at 5:51 P.M. on July 27 and another was at 8:00 A.M. *[handwritten: p.m. / a.m.]*

14

Grammar and Usage 4

Test your knowledge of grammar and usage in the following exercises. For interactive practice exercises and resources, check our Web site: *http://info.wadsworth.com/rich.*

4-1. Active vs. passive voice

Active voice is usually preferable to passive voice. Active voice means your subject is doing the action. In sentences with passive voice, the subject is the person, people or things to whom the action was done. The sentence with passive voice often contains the words *by* or *for*. In some cases, you want to use passive voice if you want to stress who received the action, but strive for active voice.

Active: Students planned a demonstration to protest tuition increases.
Passive: A demonstration was planned by students to protest tuition increases.
Active: A judge sentenced the 38-year-old bank robber to five years in prison.
Preferable passive: The 38-year-old robber was sentenced to five years in prison (if you want to stress the robber, not the judge).

Identify whether active or passive voice is used in the following sentences:

a. _____John Smith was nominated for fraternity president by Joe Chance.

b. _____Judge Raymond Burr sentenced the man convicted of drunken driving to two years in jail.

c. _____Students conducted a rally yesterday to raise money.

d. _____ The case was dismissed by a three-judge panel.

4-2. Action verbs vs. linking verbs

Verbs that express action are preferable to linking verbs (is, are, was, were) that simply link a subject to a noun or pronoun. Whenever you start a sentence with *There*, an expletive, you are forced to use a weak linking verb. For example:

Weak: There *were* 13 students who marched in the parade.
Stronger action verb: Thirteen students *marched* in the parade.
Rewrite these sentences using action verbs.

a. There was in increase in tuition costs last year in universities throughout the nation.

b. There is a demand for technology that contributed to the increased tuition.

c. There is new legislation that reduces the interest rates on federally backed student loans.

d. There are many students who need to improve their grammar skills before they can become good writers.

e. There were 17 students who attended the lecture, but there were many others who decided to stay home because of the inclement weather.

4-3. Dangling modifiers

Phrases that start with participles – verbs that end in *ing* – are used to modify nouns. They should be placed directly before the noun they modify. When they are incorrectly placed, they can be silly. They dangle. Ask yourself who is doing the action in the phrase.

Dangling phrase: Running to class, *his boot* fell off when he tripped.
His boot wasn't running to class. He was.
    Correct: Running to class, *he* tripped and his boot fell off.
    Alternative: As he was running to class, he tripped and his boot fell off.

Rewrite the following sentences to correct the dangling modifiers:

a. Carrying his books in his backpack, the strap broke.

b. When planning a meeting, an agenda is advisable.

c. While discussing the election, the topic of privacy and politicians aroused heated debate.

d. Living in a small town for many years, the large population of this city overwhelmed him.

e. After spending three hours in the library, the number of books seemed endless.

4-4. It's, Its

It's is a contraction for it is. *Its* is possessive, meaning belonging to it. If you can substitute *it is* for *it's*, the contraction is the right form. Circle the correct form.

a. (Its It's) important for you to learn the difference between these two words.

b. The dog chased (its it's) tail for hours.

c. When (its it's) time for you to graduate, you need to fill out several forms.

d. The university lost (its it's) accreditation last year.

e. The newspaper won (its it's) first Pulitzer Prize this year.

4-5. That, Which

That and *which* are two very confusing words in sentences. *That* introduces a clause that is essential to the meaning of the sentence. If the sentence is not clear without the clause, use *that* without a comma before it. If the sentence can stand alone without the clause, use *which*, preceded by a comma. Sometimes it's just a matter of interpretation.

Examples:
This is the textbook *that* you need for this course. Which book? The one you need for the course so you need *that*.

He wrote many books, *which* were bestsellers. They happened to be bestsellers, but you could probably understand the sentence without the clause.

Circle the correct usage; if you choose *which*, insert a comma before it.

a. The student production of *Macbeth* (which that) is the third play the drama club is planning this year, will be in March.

b. This is the test (which that) you must take on Monday.

c. Alaska (which that) is the 49th state, is one of the most beautiful states in the nation.

d. The basketball team (which that) had many freshmen players this year, made it to the Final Four.

e. The computer lab (which that) contains the Macintosh computers, was vandalized.

4-6. Who or Whom

Who is the subject of a sentence or clause, meaning *who* does the action. Whom is the object; it receives the action. The confusion occurs in clauses, such as she is the person *whom* I called. I called *whom.* Substitute *him* or *her* for *whom* and see if it makes sense when you turn the clause or sentence around. *Who* is equivalent to *I, he* or *she.*

a. The person (who whom) is in charge of hiring is the one who whom you should contact.

b. (Who Whom) do you plan to see when you go for your job interview?

c. These are the officials (who whom) will make the decision about whether your organization gets the money.

d. Do you know (who whom) is in charge of the event?

e. I don't know (who whom) was responsible but (whoever or whomever stole the fraternity mascot will be caught.

4-7. Run-on sentences

When two complete sentences are joined by a comma, they are called "run-on" sentences or "comma splices." Use a period or a semicolon if the two sentences are very closely related in thought. A period is always a safe choice. You may also use conjunctions such as *and, but, or, for, nor* preceded by a comma. Determine whether these sentences are run-on sentences or are correct. Fix them if they are incorrect.

a. You may pay your tuition with a credit card, it's a new university policy.

b. Many states are trying to pass legislation to make English the only permissible language for government business, a policy that several Spanish-speaking groups oppose.

c. The election was highly contested, the candidates were glad when it was over.

d. A fire during a Halloween dance was one of the deadliest fires in Sweden, at least 62 people were killed.

e. More than 60 people were killed, 173 others were injured, when flames erupted in the dance hall filled with teen-agers.

4-8. Subject-verb agreement

18

A singular subject such as *each, neither, either, every, everyone,* must take a singular verb. Likewise a plural subject takes a plural verb. The agreement can be tricky if a phrase or clause follows the word. For example: *Each* one of the women *is* going to play on the team. Ignore the phrase *of the women.* Choose the correct verb:

a. Every one of the players is are getting new sneakers.

b. Each of the students expects expect to get an A.

c. Three quarters of the students are is failing the course.

d. Either the professor or the graduate assistant is are going to bring the test.

e. Everybody in this program want wants to get a job.

4-9. General usage

Test your knowledge of usage covered in your textbook. Choose the correct item:

a. The media is are often blamed for poor coverage of politics.

b. The student felt bad badly after she took the test.

c. I am eager anxious to get a new job.

d. He thought it was alright all right to turn his paper in a few days late.

e. The Board of Education met last night, and they it plan plans to resume

discussion of the proposal next week.

f. Some people thought the president's behavior was

embarrassing embarassing.

g. Each of the board members know knows what he or she they must do.

h. How much further farther do we have to go before we reach the lake?

i. If I was were in your position, I would quit.

j. None of the women in the class were was planning to go on to graduate school.

k. It's clear that the argument was between he him and his wife.

l. The date for submitting the advertising campaign was not going to work out for either he him or his boss.

m. Give the free pizza to whoever whomever shows up first.

n. Do you know who whom hit the most home runs?

o. You never know who whom you will run into when you go to the cafe.

p. I know I laid lay lied the book on the table last night, but it disappeared.

q. You should have used better judgment judgement.

r. None of you is are going to graduate this spring.

s. He was planning to become a restauranteur restaurateur.

t. The journalism school, which that is on K Street, is the building with the green roof.

u. Whom Who did you send your resume to when you mailed it last week?

v. If you lose loose the election, you can run again next semester.

w. If I was were in a better mood, I'd let you skip this test.

x. Less Fewer than five students showed up for the presentation.

y. The disagreement is strictly between you and I you and me, so I don't think you should ask your brother to intervene.

z. If you studied alot a lot of these items in your textbook, you should do well.

Curiosity and Story Ideas 5

Your senses of sight and sound are important reporting tools. To a lesser degree, what you smell, touch and taste also can provide information for your story. This chapter is intended to help you learn how to use your curiosity and observation to report and write news stories. Although much of your information for news stories comes from answers sources give to your questions, what you see, hear, and smell at a scene may also be included in a story. Your observations will generate information for the writing technique known as "show-in-action," meaning you can show what your sources are doing as well as tell what they say.

These exercises also are designed to help you develop ways of thinking about story ideas. Although many story ideas at newspapers, magazines, television stations and corporations are conceived and assigned by editors or department supervisors, reporters and public relations practitioners are expected to suggest their own ideas as well. Remember to include ideas for visual presentation with your story ideas. Search the Internet for background or other related ideas.

You may link directly to many sites for this chapter on our Web site for this book: *http://info.wadsworth.com/rich*.

5-1. Coaching

Pair up with a partner in the class and coach each other on a story idea for a news or feature story you plan to write.

Coaching questions:
- What is the main idea of your story? Answer in one sentence.
- What is new about this story?
- What is the "so-what" factor? What makes this story newsworthy now?
- Is there anything in this story that is unusual, helpful or informative, such as news about a trend or material that is consumer-oriented?
- What effect will this story have on readers? What makes this story of interest to your readers?

5-2. Three ideas in 15 minutes

This is a quick class exercise you can do in 15 minutes if you are located in or near a campus building with bulletin boards. Find at least three ideas for news stories by looking at fliers on bulletin boards, checking with students in other departments or observing anything newsworthy on campus. Then return to class and write your ideas as new briefs – about three or four paragraphs for each idea.

5-3. A-Z brainstorming

Working alone or in groups, make a list of nouns from A to Z that you will use to generate story ideas. Or, if your instructor prefers, each student can take one or a few letters of the alphabet. For example: A for accident or agriculture, B for bike paths in your community or campus, C for cold – the illness or the weather, F for fear, and so forth. Share some of these words with the class. Then brainstorm story ideas that you can apply to your campus or community for development into news or feature stories. This exercise was conceived by Kathy English, a former journalism professor in Canada. She calls it a "dictionary of subjects." If you are struggling to think of good topic words, you could consult your dictionary for ideas.

5-4. Localize national news

You are the editor of your campus newspaper. You are scanning the wire service and find the following national stories. How would you localize them for your campus newspaper? Write a few sentences to develop the local angle for each issue, identifying experts or leaders of groups on campus and in your community whom you would interview.

a. The U.S. Department of Labor released a study predicting that from now through the first few years of the 21st century, the number of college graduates would exceed the number of jobs to match their skills. The report said that about 25 percent of the 25 million college graduates in the last year were working in jobs that did not require the degrees they held. The report predicted that by the year 2005, 78 percent of all the jobs available will not require a college degree and that 30 percent of all college graduates would take a job for which they were overqualified.

b. Next week is National Coming Out Day, a day dedicated to encouraging gays and lesbians to accept their sexual orientation and to discourage discrimination.

c. Check CNN and MSNBC for news stories. Localize three of them for your community. CNN: *www.cnn.com;* MSNBC: *www.msnbc.com.*

5-5. Special sections

Brainstorm ideas for the following special sections:

a. Your campus newspaper is planning a special section about fashion, primarily aimed at male and female college students. Plan at least five story ideas that would appeal to this audience.

b. Your campus newspaper is planning a special section about entertainment for college students. The section will feature ideas about places or entertainers in your community, such as local bands, restaurants, bars and nightclubs, and other recreational activities that students would enjoy. Plan at least five story ideas for such a section.

5-6. Classified advertisements

Read the following classified advertisements that appeared in campus newspapers, and identify newsworthy angles for a story in your campus newspaper. (Each ad was followed by a phone number.) Discuss or write a budget line identifying sources you might contact and a focus you would develop.

a. Need cash? Help others while helping yourself. We need men and women to donate valuable plasma. We provide TV entertainment, two hours free parking, $15 for each donation.

b. Therapeutic hypnosis. Gentle, non-coercive, holistic. Also therapeutic Tarot readings for problem solving, insight. Certified hypnotherapist.

5-7. Plan an online newspaper

Plan an online newspaper for your campus or community. If you already have one, plan how you might improve it or develop a competing online site. Working individually or in small groups, brainstorm the kinds of stories and online features you would include in your publication. If you are working in groups, divide the responsibilities for sections in your newspaper. For example, you could have the following editors: city editor responsible for local news, sports editor, business editor, national/foreign news editor and a lifestyle/entertainment editor. What interactive elements would you include such as forums, chats, games, discussion questions? Then write a plan explaining your concepts.

Consider the following questions:
- What features in your online publication would differ from a print publication?
- What kinds of stories or interactive features would appeal to the demographic groups in your market? Are there special groups you would try to reach, such as high school students? Would you include more news of interest to women and minorities, and if so, what kinds of stories would you suggest?

- Don't forget to brainstorm the interactive features you would include.
- What topics would lend themselves to reader participation?

5-8. Curiosity training

Imagine that you are a reporter and your editor gives you the following assignments with only this limited information. What questions can you brainstorm for each incident? Write at least five questions for each scenario.

a. A man has been shot in a local bar that is a popular student hangout.
b. Two people have been injured in a three-car crash on a main street in your community.
c. Minority students on your campus are staging a protest.

5-9. Descriptive writing from observation

Write a few descriptive paragraphs based on this premise: You have been missing for a week, and a reporter has come to your apartment, home or room to write about your disappearance. The story might start as follows: The room was just as she or he left it. Use only those details that reveal your personality or habits. Use specific details; avoid vague adjectives.

5-10. Analogies

Write analogies (a simile using like or as or a metaphor comparing one item with another without using like or as) for items on your campus or general items such as: snow, summer, Dumpster, a person you know, sunset, and so on. For example, an analogy would be: The snow covered the earth like a blanket of cotton candy. A metaphor would be: The snow was a blanket of cotton candy covering the earth.

Sources and Online Research 6

The Internet has become a valuable resource for journalists who can check background, statistics and many facts online. But if you are searching for articles from newspapers and magazines, many of these online publications charge for access to their archived stories. Your campus and local libraries are still important sources for research. Most libraries now have a wide variety of information on databases, which are very easy to use. You should familiarize yourself with these resources. You can link directly to several online sites from the Web site for this book: *http://info.wadsworth.com/rich*.

6-1. Sources: Terminology

Define the following terms:

a. On the record_____

b. Off the record_____

c. Background_____

d. Deep background _____

e. What did the U.S. Supreme Court rule in the Dan Cohen case against the (Minneapolis) *Star Tribune?*

_____

6-2. Web site credibility

List five factors you should consider to check the credibility of Web sites:

1._____

2._____

3._____

4._____

5._____

6-3. Online sources

1. You are writing a story about the growing use plagiarism on college campuses and you want to include information about a site that professors may use to check students' papers for plagiarism. What is the name of the site and its URL (site address)?

    _____

2. You have the environmental beat and you are writing a story about hazardous wastes in your community. Find resources from the Society of Environmental Journalists and list the URL.

    _____

3. You have just gotten a job at Newsday in Long Island, N.Y. and you have been assigned to cover Nassau County. Using the 2000 U.S. Census, find the following information:
    a. Percent of population change from 1990-2000_____
    b. Percent of people over 65 years old _____
    c. Percent of black or African American persons in 2000_____

4. You are writing a story on sexually transmitted diseases for your campus newspaper. You have heard that chlamydia is the fastest growing disease in this category. Find a reliable government source for information and answer these questions. **Clue:** Centers for Disease Control.
    a. What is chlamydia?_____

    b. How many cases are estimated to occur annually in the United States?

        _____

5. You are writing a report about cyberterrorism. Go to yearbook.com and find an expert on this subject:

    _____

6. You are writing a story about job prospects in the future, and you want to know which occupations will grow the most by the year 2010. Check the U.S. Department of Labor projections for the occupations and list the three occupations that will experience the largest job growth from 2000 to 2010.
    a. _____
    b. _____
    b. _____

7. You want to find obituaries of some famous people. Check obituary.com and answer these questions. To start your research, use a directory and answer these questions:

    a. Who is the creator of Donald Duck? _____

    b. When did he die and what was the cause?_____

    c. Who was William Randolph Hearst's lover?_____

    d. What movie did Hearst try to prevent? _____

8. Almanacs are great sources for statistics and other information journalists need to include background or perspective in a story. Information Please almanac offers this information online *www.infoplease.com/*. Using this online source find answers to the following questions:

    a. You are writing a story about presidential sex scandals. What scandal involved President Grover Cleveland?

_____

Top three coaches.

    b. Who are the top three coaches who have won the most NCAA basketball tournaments?

_____

9. You are writing a story about global warming and how it affects Antarctica. How much of this continent is covered by ice? **Clue:** Check the CIA World Facts Book.

_____

10. You are considering a job in a new city and you want to compare the cost of living. Find a free site that offers comparisons. What is the salary difference for a person who makes $50,000 and is moving from Kansas City, Mo., to San Francisco, Calif.? **Clue:** Try a search for salary calculators or try these sites: monster moving, homefair or virtual relocation.

_____

Interviewing Techniques 7

Do you struggle writing full quotes in your notes when you interview sources? Are you thinking of what you will say rather than listening to what the source says? The exercises in the first part of this chapter are designed to help you identify your problems and improve your concentration so you can take better notes. The second set of exercises will reinforce your interviewing skills.

For more resources on this subject, check the Web site for this book: *http://info.wadsworth.com/rich.*

7-1. Your listening profile

The prerequisite for taking good notes is good listening. This is an unscientific test. It is meant only to help you identify your strengths and weaknesses in listening skills. Rate yourself for your listening skills by circling the answer that best describes you.

a. On a scale of 1 to 10 (1= terrible to 10 = excellent) rate yourself as a listener.

    1   2   3   4   5   6   7   8   9   10

b. On a scale of 1 to 10, (1= terrible to 10 = excellent) how do you think your friends would you rate you as a listener?

    1   2   3   4   5   6   7   8   9   10

c. When you are talking with friends, do you interrupt?

    Often   Sometimes   Rarely   Never

d. When you receive instructions verbally in a class, how often do you need to have them repeated so you understand them?

> Often   Sometimes   Rarely   Never

e. When you listen to your favorite songs with words, how often do you know the score by heart?

> Often   Sometimes   Rarely   Never

f. When you are in your lecture classes, what factors inhibit your listening skills?

> (1) Boredom
> (2) Thoughts of personal problems
> (3) Difficulty hearing
> (4) Lack of interest in the subject matter
> (5) Limited attention span
> (6) Other
> (7) None of the above

g. When you are conversing with your friends, what factors inhibit your listening skills?

> (1) Boredom
> (2) Thoughts of personal problems
> (3) Difficulty hearing
> (4) Lack of interest in the subject matter
> (5) Limited attention span
> (6) Other
> (7) None of the above

h. When you are interviewing a source for a story, what factors inhibit your listening skills?

> (1) Boredom
> (2) Thoughts of personal problems
> (3) Difficulty hearing
> (4) Lack of interest in the subject matter
> (5) Limited attention span
> (6) Other
> (7) None of the above

i. When you are interviewing a source for a story, how often do you concentrate more on what you are going to ask next instead of what the source is saying?

Often Sometimes Rarely Never

j. Now look at the answers you have circled. Do you notice any patterns? Are you thinking about personal problems or questions you might ask when you are conversing with friends or sources? Is your major problem a limited attention span, indicating lack of concentration or boredom? Using these answers as a guide or others that characterize your listening habits, identify your weaknesses:

I need to work on improving my listening skills by overcoming:

_____ _____

_____ _____

_____ _____

_____ _____

7-2. Interviewing

Now test your skills in a real situation. Pair up with a classmate and conduct a brief interview about any subject of interest to you or any controversy on campus. For example, you could ask your classmate's opinion about grades, requirements for your major, music preferences, experiences students had in study abroad programs (if applicable), concerns about graduation or getting a job, and so forth. The point is to get as many good direct quotes as you can. Also take notes on basic information – the person's hometown, birth date and other biographical data – so you can test your recall. Just do this very briefly, about five or 10 minutes. Read back what direct quotes you have taken, and ask the student if that sounds accurate. Then switch roles. Chances are the student won't remember exactly what he or she said, but your classmate will be able to test the accuracy of other information in your notes.

7-3. Concentration

If you want to remember quotes from your sources, you have to concentrate when you hear them. Test your concentration skills:

a. Read one of these two paragraphs quickly. Then turn the book over or cover it with a piece of paper. Try to write it as exactly as you can. (Alternative method: Pair up with a partner in your class. Ask your partner to read one of these two   selections to you. Then write as much of the selection you heard as accurately you can.) After you have completed your portion, read the next selection to your partner.

These passages are from *The World Is My Home: A Memoir* by James Michener, Random House, 1992.

"I am always interested in why young people become writers, and from talking with many I have concluded that most do not want to be writers working eight and ten hours a day and accomplishing little; they want to *have been* writers, garnering the rewards of having completed a successful manuscript, and seeing it become a best-seller. They aspire to the rewards of writing, but not to the travail." (p. 349)

"If I were a young writer today starting over, I would focus my attention on the changing relationships between the sexes; despite my age I am fascinated by this and the other subjects but do not feel myself qualified to write about them." (p. 507.)

b. This is a famous passage from "Hamlet" by William Shakespeare. Read it quickly and then cover it or turn the book over. Write it as exactly as you can.

To be, or not to be, that is the question:
Whether 'tis nobler in the mind to suffer
The slings and arrows of outrageous fortune,
Or to take arms against a sea of troubles
And by opposing end them. To die: to sleep
No more; and by a sleep to say we end
The heart-ache and the thousand natural shocks
That flesh is heir to: 'tis a consummation
Devoutly to be wish'd.

7-4. Coaching

Pair up with a classmate and take turns coaching each other on a story that you are planning to use for a class assignment. Coach each other on the idea and on other phases of the story. If you are coaching before the interview has been conducted, brainstorm some questions with your partner. If you are coaching after the interview, use the suggested questions for writing guidance. Your role as the coach is to ask guiding questions and to listen to your partner's answers. If you don't have someone to coach you, try to answer these questions yourself before you do your interview. Here are some coaching questions, but you may add more:

Coaching on the idea:

1. What is the story about? Answer in one or two sentences.
2. What is the focus?
3. What's the point – the "so-what" factor?
4. Why are you writing about this now? Is there a timeliness factor?
5. What's new, unusual, different, helpful or indicative of a pattern/trend in this story?
6. If this idea is for a feature about some previous event, what makes it newsworthy now?
7. What effect, if any, will this story have on readers? Why would they want to be informed about this topic?
8. What strikes you as interesting about this topic?

Coaching for the interview:

1. What are the main points the reader needs to know to understand this issue?
2. Do you have sources to confirm, react or provide other points of view? What sources should you contact?
3. Do you have background about the person or issue? Is there any previous related story you should check?
4. What do you want to know? (The coach can add some questions here.)
5. What difficulties are you anticipating? Do you have any alternative ways of getting this information?

Coaching after the interview:

1. What struck you as most interesting in the interview? Was it related to the focus?
2. Do you have enough information to back up your focus? If not, should you change your focus?
3. What interesting anecdotes or facts did you learn from the interview?

For the writer: If you are still struggling with your focus, try writing a hard-news lead; that lead could be your nut graph if you plan to use a soft lead.

7-5. Observing interviewing techniques

Work in groups of three. One person will be an observer while the other two interview each other. Then switch, letting the observer be an interviewer and so on until each person has had a chance to be an observer. While you are observing, do not say anything. Just jot down notes about the interviewer's techniques. You may fill out the following sheet or just use it to guide you. When you are finished interviewing each other, discuss the strengths and weaknesses you noticed. Analyze your own interviewing weaknesses and strengths. You could watch a news show that features interviews and use the following form to rate the broadcaster doing the interview.

Observer's Form – Reporting Techniques

Rate the interviewer on the following traits by circling the appropriate adjectives:

1. Manner (pleasantness, politeness, friendliness)......... Good   Fair   Poor

2. Eye contact with the source..................................... Good   Fair   Poor

3. Interviewer's interest in subject............................... Good   Fair   Poor

4. Quality of the questions.. Good   Fair   Poor

5. Listening skills.. Good   Fair   Poor

6. Control of interview .... Good   Fair   Poor

7. Note-taking skills.. Good   Fair   Poor

8. List the interviewer's strengths:

9. Briefly describe the interviewer's weaknesses.

10. What recommendations do you have for the interviewer?

7-6. E-mail interview

Plan an e-mail interview. Jot down your most crucial questions before you write them. Interviews by e-mail should contain only a few questions. You might want to try first interviewing a classmate by e-mail before you do this with a source. Discuss how your e-mail interview compares with telephone or face-to-face interviewing. What are the pros and cons of e-mail interviewing?

7-7. Interview a news source

Interview a source who has been in the news or one who frequently deals with the media. The purpose of your interview is to ask the source about his or her experiences with the media. You are responsible for learning some background about your source. You will need to ask follow-up questions, and you should seek specific examples of good and bad experiences the source has had with the media. For example, if your source says some person or some newspaper or television station never treats him or her fairly, get examples of what the source means – questions asked, specific stories, and so on. After you conduct your interview, write a report (make sure you include background about your source). To encourage candor from your source, you may tell the source this report is for a class assignment and not for publication. Here are some questions to guide you:

1. How often do you come in contact with the media?

2. With whom are your contacts (local newspaper and radio, regional newspapers and TV, state media, national media)?

3. How long have you had press contact? Is it steady or intermittent?

4. Have you had other roles in the past in which you had press coverage? Please explain.

5. Have you been interviewed primarily for hard news or feature stories?

6. Are most of your interviews in person or by telephone? Which do you prefer and why?

7. Do you ever contact the press? Why or why not? Give examples, if you do.

8. Overall, how do you view your coverage by the media so far (fair, accurate, complete)? Please specify if the coverage differs for newspapers, radio, television or magazines.

9. Have you had bad experiences with interviewers? Would you cite examples of interviewing techniques and reporting that you considered bad interviewing techniques? (Here you will need to seek specifics from your source for the most complete explanation you can get.) Have you experienced poorly stated or ignorant questions, misinterpretation of your position, inaccurate quotes, personality conflict with the interviewer or bias by the interviewer?

10. In situations in which you might not have been presented as positively as you would have liked, was the coverage fair and accurate? Explain.

11. Do you have any general complaints about interviews?

12. If you were involved in any good interviews, what made them good? Did the interviewer do something new that you thought made him or her more effective?

13. What suggestions about interviewing do you have for beginning reporters?

7-8. Beyond the 5 W's

By now you know that basic news stories contain the answers to who, what, when, where, why, how and so what. But those simple questions can be far more revealing if you expand on each element. For example, what is entailed in finding information for the questions who and what? Does that include the person's background, likes and dislikes, and so forth? Brainstorm as many questions as you can for each of those basic elements. This exercise is adapted from one developed by Donald Murray, who is considered the father of the writing coach movement and is author of several books about writing. Here are some sample questions to get you started:

Who: Full name including middle name or initial, nickname if any, age, sex, address, occupation. Be specific and include where the person works, special skills, likes, dislikes, hobbies.

What: Specifics of what happened, what happened before this event, what followed event, what was said or felt, what is the impact, sequence of events.

When: Day, month, year, how often, how long did experience last, specific time of incident, how often or rarely does this occur.

Where: Street, city, county, state, country, building, unusual or common facts about the building or place, size of place, atmosphere including sound, smell.

Why: Winners, losers, reasons, why now, what led up to event, what will transpire because of it, what might have prevented it, what inspired it, what changes will result.

How: Who or what inspired incident, sequence of event (also under what), how many people involved, what led to event, specific forces that contributed.

So what: Who or what is affected, what stays the same or changes, results, area involved, people involved, next step.

7-9. Dissect a newspaper story

Read a newspaper story and dissect it by writing the questions you think the reporter asked to get the information. Then discuss or write additional questions you think the reporter should have asked.

The Writing Process

The exercises in this chapter will give you practice organizing, tightening and revising stories and following Associated Press style. You also will get a chance to plan a process for presenting a story on the Web.

8-1. FORK exercise

Organize this story by using the basic FORK method. First read all the notes, find your focus and write that at the top of your story. Then jot down a basic order for the story, blocking all the material from each source. Because this is a feature story, there is no single correct way to organize the information. Put it in an order that makes sense and avoids unnatural transitions. Also avoid stringing many quotes together. Consider a lead that starts with a story about one person and then proceeds to the nut graph. Or try a creative lead based on the topic. If the information is not enclosed in quotation marks, the comments are not direct quotes.

General notes:

Nutritionists agree it's understandable that students who stay up late to study need to eat to keep going. In their newsletters, nutritionists suggest that fruit or even pretzels would be healthier snacks than candy or pizza.

The fabled Freshman 15 affects men and women, according to students. Those nasty 10 to 15 pounds that students tend to gain in the first few months of college have become as much a part of higher education as reading lists and blue-book exams.

Many schools send new students another helpful message during orientation: Find time between study and socializing to exercise every day, be it through sports, aerobics classes or a simple walk. Some schools, such as the University of Pennsylvania and Rutgers University, offer special workshops to freshmen to help them avoid the weight gain.

Gene Lamm, a junior at Beaver College in Glenside: "I've gained 20 pounds since I left home." He made the comment as he shared an entire chocolate cake with two friends. "I used to have abs (abdominal muscles); I don't know what happened to them," Lamm said, chuckling, as he lifted his gray T-shirt.

Peg Abell, a nutritionist at Widener University: Often students eat out of stress and even more often in an effort to socialize and fit in. "Some people eat to feel better since eating can have a soothing effect, and some use eating as a way of maintaining control of at least one portion of their life."

Joe Leung, a junior at Villanova: "I went up for second portions every day. I weighed 115 when I came, and I got up to 140."

Missy Palko, a sophomore at Beaver College: "I gained 30 pounds last year. If you look in the closets around here, they're all packed with food."

An informal survey of dorm residents proved her right. Room after room held stashes of cheese crackers, doughnuts, popcorn, frosted breakfast cereals, chocolate and sodas.

Vanessa Varvarezis, a freshman who had been at Villanova only three weeks at the time of this interview: "I think I've already gained it. My parents sent me away with four bags of junk food, and it's almost half gone already."

Eating at Donahue Hall one recent evening, Varvarezis had spaghetti, garlic bread, vegetables, about eight cookies and a fudge ice cream pop. "It was Weight Watchers, though," she said about the dessert.

According to a calorie chart given out by the Villanova food services staff, Varvarezis had eaten more than 900 calories for dinner. And that was before the late-night pizza run. "I order out a lot," Varvarezis said. "Grease, grease, lots of grease."

Jim Martin, manager of California Style Pizza, near Villanova University: "We call them the pie hours." From 9 p.m. to 2 a.m., he said, his six employees deliver up to 50 pizzas per hour to the nearby campus. He routinely makes four extra pizzas for them to take along and sell on the spot. He said his delivery people have no trouble "hawking pizzas."

Craig Zabransky, a Villanova freshman: He was at Donahue Hall, eating dinner. "Well, I'm not having nightmares about it," he said, as he dug into a generous spaghetti dinner and his fourth piece of buttery garlic bread. "I'm just going to exercise more. I'm going to start tomorrow."

Stephen Bailey, a sociology professor who conducted a weight-gain study for Tufts University in Massachusetts with Tufts nutrition professor Jeanne Goldberg: They tracked 120 women through their first year of college. He said the Freshman 15 is "a myth."

"Basically we came up with some results that surprised us. On average, the women gained a little bit less than a pound. They gained a bit between the fall and spring and lost all of that over the course of the summer." The participants were volunteers.

Adapted from a story in *The Philadelphia Inquirer.* Used with permission.

8-2. Revision to tighten and correct style

This story has many extraneous words and style errors. Before you submit your stories to your editor or professor, you should revise them by checking for accuracy and tightening your writing, as in this exercise. Edit or rewrite this story by eliminating wordiness and correcting style errors.

A woman named Shirley Anne Hall has up until December 8 to clear up her Garden Grove house of rotten oranges that have gone bad, cobwebs, vehicle parts, musty newspapers and a year's worth of dirty dishes that have not been washed.

Hall, who is age 54, must remove overgrown weeds in her yard and other debris from her yard, which is located in the 12,000 block of Barlett Street, Orange County, superior court judge Randell Wilkinson said on Wednsday. If she fails to comply with the order which judge Randell Wilkinson made on Wednesday, the city will bring in work crews and send Hall the bill for the work the crews have done.

The city has been trying to persuade Hall to sort through her mess since the year of 1988, city attorney Stuart Scudder said.

Hall, a woman who is diagnosed with chronic depression, said the city is harrassing her and that the stress that the city has caused her by harrassing her has prevented her from making any progress.

The Dayle McIntosh Center for the Disabled in Anaheim is looking for volunteers who of their own volition will offer to help Hall to clean up.

Adapted from a story in *The Orange County* (Calif.) *Register.* Used with permission.

8-3. Style test

The first part of this exercise involves active and passive voice and the second part is a test of Associated Press style. Rewrite these sentences as directed.

Part 1. Change these sentences from passive to active voice. In some cases passive voice is preferable. Which do you prefer in these sentences?

1. Fourteen months later in the fall of 1986, a marriage proposal came from Bob Goldman in the form of a diamond ring tucked inside a fortune cookie.
2. Expectations by Barbara Wasserman and Bob Goldman that their blind date would work out were low.
3. A speech was given by Christopher Carter, an officer in a public relations firm.
4. A 24-year-old man was arrested last night and charged with possession of an illegal substance by police.
5. A survey of students to determine weight gain among college freshmen was conducted by two university professors.

Part II. Circle and correct the style errors in these sentences.

6. Stephen Bailey, a sociology professor, says the idea that freshmen gain fifteen lbs. is "a myth".
7. Women gained a little bit less than 1 pound, between Fall and Spring but they lost it during the Summer.
8. Barbara Wasserman met her future fiancé by the dumpster.
9. She said its a good thing that she decided to go on the blind date.
10. Lamm lifted his tee-shirt to reveal his expanding stomach.
11. Amy Jaffee, a 29-year-old journalist, says most romances that are arranged fizzle after the 2nd or 3rd date.
12. From 9 P.M. to 2 A.M. Jim Martin delivers up to fifty pizzas to Villanova University students.
13. 120 women were surveyed for the weight-gain study.
14. Nathaniel Branden said, "Its predictable and inevitable that we would see a resurgence of blind dating".
15. Gene Lamm said he gained twenty lbs. during his freshman year of college.

Leads and Nut Graphs

9

The following exercises will give you practice writing a variety of leads. Before you write your lead you should identify the focus of the story. If you want to write a soft lead, your focus should be your nut graph. If you think the story should have a hard-news lead, your focus should be in your lead. You may find it helpful to write a focus sentence before you write your lead. Instead of struggling to write the perfect lead, try writing several leads and then choose one you prefer. Check the book's Web site for direct links to resources: *http://info.wadsworth.com/rich*

9-1. Hard-news (summary) leads

These leads summarize the main point of the story. Choose the most important elements of who, what, where, when, why or how, but don't clutter your lead with all these elements. Place points of emphasis (the most interesting or important information) at the beginning of the sentence. Read the following information, and write a one-sentence summary lead for each item.

1. A survey was released yesterday by the Child Abuse Prevention Center in Baltimore. The survey shows that three to four children die every day in the United States from child abuse or neglect. Statistics in the survey show that the number of child abuse or neglect cases reported at the end of this year rose to 2.7 million, from 2.5 million the previous year. More than half of the children who died were under age 1. Seventy-nine percent of the deaths were among children under age 5.

2. MILWAUKEE – For the past three days nearly 2,500 people have been demonstrating outside of an abortion clinic here. Some demonstrators support the clinic and others oppose it. Yesterday nearly 150 of the anti-abortion protesters were arrested. Police said they were arrested on disorderly conduct charges of blocking the entrances to the clinic. The protesters said they planned to demonstrate for six weeks. (Clue: Avoid starting with a numeral.)

3. This information comes from police. A delivery driver for a Chinese food restaurant was taking food to an apartment in your town yesterday. The apartment complex was at 718 S.W. Western Ave. The driver was robbed of the Chinese food at gunpoint. The driver works for The Great Wall of China Restaurant at 1336 S.W. 17th St. A man opened the outside security door for him to let him in, and then the man disappeared. A short time later, the man came back and pointed a gun at the delivery driver. The man threatened to kill the driver unless he handed over the food. The driver gave it to him and ran out of the apartment building. Police weren't sure what specific food dishes the driver was carrying.

4. A fire in your town caused $45,000 in damages to a two-bedroom home in the 2300 block of Main Street. Fire officials said the fire was started by a lighted cigarette on a sofa. Firefighters arrived at the house at 3:30 a.m. and found it on fire. They had the blaze under control in five minutes. The homeowner, Kathy Mahoney, was awakened by the smoke and flames. She suffered minor burns on her hands and feet.

5. The state Bureau of Investigation [in your state] yesterday released a report of crime rates for the first three months of the year. The report says murders in your state are up 53 percent and violent crime increased 2 percent. The state bureau officials said the number of rapes and robberies decreased significantly.

6. A United Nations scientific panel released a report yesterday. Researchers of the United Nations Environment Program found that damage to the earth's ozone layer is increasing. They predicted that ozone levels could drop 3 percent in the next decade, which would lead to a 10-percent increase in skin cancer. The ozone layer above the earth absorbs some of the sun's cancer-causing ultraviolet rays.

7. Information comes from police in Santa Ana, Calif. A Santa Ana woman was charged with attempted murder yesterday. She was being held in the Orange County jail after being unable to post $250,000 bond. Police said the woman, June Carter, 71, doused her husband, who was confined to a wheelchair and had cancer, with rubbing alcohol and set him on fire. Police said she was angry because he ate her chocolate Easter bunny. She called paramedics six hours after the attack on her husband. Paul Carter, 62, was taken to the University of California Irvine Burn Center with third-degree burns, police said.

9-2. Delayed identification leads

When the person in your lead is not well known, you can delay identifying him or her until the second paragraph. Instead of using a name in the lead, you can identify the person by age, occupation (or affiliation with a group), location or some description. Write delayed identification leads as directed.

1. *Use age as your delayed identification factor.* Use your city as the location and yesterday as your time frame. Information comes from police. Police said John Cryer's tears may have saved him. Cryer was 13. He was walking in the 2700 block of S.E. 10th St. about 5:25 p.m. when a car containing four people pulled alongside. The driver displayed a blue semiautomatic handgun and demanded the boy's jacket. The boy was wearing a Chicago Bulls jacket. The boy started crying. The driver said, "Never mind," and the car left. No one was hurt or arrested.

Based on a story from *The Topeka Capital-Journal.* Used with permission.

2. *Use occupation or organization affiliation as your delayed identification factor.* Mike Haney spoke at your university yesterday. He is a founder of the American Indian Movement. He urged the audience to support a ban on using Indian names and symbols as mascots in sports. He said that using Indians as mascots promotes racism. "If all the kids see are those guys out there in the parking lot with makeup on their faces and dyed chicken feathers doing the war whoop, or they just see those TV westerns, that's how they'll perceive us," he said.

Based on a story from *The Topeka Capital-Journal.* Used with permission.

3. *Use location as your delayed identification factor.* John Sony, 69, was in critical condition at St. Francis Hospital and Medical Center yesterday. He is from Emporia (or use your town). He was diagnosed with Legionnaires' disease, which state health officials suspect he contracted at his high school reunion. Legionnaires' disease can cause a severe form of pneumonia. The disease was first identified in 1976 when 34 people died after attending an American Legion convention in a Philadelphia hotel.

Based on a story from *The Topeka Capital-Journal.* Used with permission.

4. *Use a descriptive identifier for delayed identification.* Information is from police reports. A man unsuccessfully tried to rob an eastside grocery store with a handgun last night. The man was wearing a white sack over his face. He entered the store and demanded money from the cashier at Food 4 Less at 3110 S.E. 6th. St. The cashier leaned against the alarm button. The suspect fled but was captured within an hour. He is Jack Fastrun of 2500 Easy St. He was charged with attempted robbery.

5. *Use occupation or location for delayed identification.* Audrey Feline, 50, a former animal control police officer (use your town), was arrested after authorities found 67 dead cats in her home. Police said the dead cats were in the woman's refrigerator and freezer. She was charged with 67 counts of misdemeanor animal abandonment.

9-3. Second-day leads

Second-day leads give a forward spin to the news by stressing what is happening now or what will happen next instead of what happened yesterday. Writing this way is also called "advancing" the lead, and this technique is almost always used in broadcast journalism. Using the following information, write second-day leads.

1. The faculty senate voted to require all undergraduates at your school to take courses in cultural diversity. The requirement goes into effect next fall and will begin with the freshman class.

2. (Use a delayed identification as well as an advance lead.) Police report that a man in your town was stabbed in a convenience store in your town last night. He is in fair condition at the hospital in your town today. Police said that Aristide Roberto, 43, was shopping in the Stop and Shop on 450 Elm St. at 2 a.m. last night when a man wearing a jogging suit stabbed him and fled. The assailant has not been found.

3. A 24-year-old Fairbanks man was shot by a state trooper who returned fire in an early morning incident, state troopers said. The man, James Risky, was out on parole after being sentenced to five years in prison for pulling a loaded gun on three police officers. In today's incident, the trooper ordered Risky to get out of a stolen car and Risky fired a shot at him, troopers said. The trooper then fired back. Risky is in critical condition in a Fairbanks hospital.

4. A Santana High School freshman opened fire with a revolver, killing two students and wounding another 13 people Monday. The 15-year-old boy later surrendered to police officers without incident. He will be arraigned as an adult in San Diego Superior Court on Wednesday. He is being charged with first-degree murder.

5. An American Airlines flight was delayed more than three hours before takeoff Sunday after a fake grenade used to test security screening fell out of a carry-on bag and rolled down the aisle, an airport spokeswoman said. A woman was in custody and authorities were trying to determine how she ended up with a bag belonging to a security screener that contained the phony grenade, said Rita Vandergaw, spokeswoman for the Unified Port of San Diego.

9-4. Impact leads

An impact lead tells readers how the story will affect them. Sometimes you may use the word "you" in your lead to personalize the impact, but you also can use a noun, such as "residents" or "voters" or whoever will be affected by the action in the story. Write impact leads for the following information.

1. The U.S. Army Corps of Engineers is conducting a program to install free plastic covering for roofs of homes damaged during the recent hurricane. There are five more days to apply for the program. Homeowners whose roofs were damaged during the storm may sign up for the free roof repair at any of the corps offices.

2. Topeka City Council is considering an ordinance to outlaw parking of vehicles in front yards and unpaved side yards. The ordinance would allow vehicles to be parked on private property only if they are on asphalt or concrete driveways. If residents have a gravel driveway, they would be forced to park in the street if the ordinance is adopted. Councilwoman Carol Schimmel, like more than 50 percent of the homeowners in her district, has a gravel driveway. She is opposed to the ordinance. "Where am I supposed to park my car?" she said. The council took the ordinance under consideration and will discuss it again at its next meeting.
Based on a story from *The Topeka Capital-Journal.* Used with permission.

3. The Missouri Board of Curators approved a new tuition rate for the University of Missouri. The tuition will increase 12 percent. That's equivalent to $240 more a year. The increase affects students at all four campuses of the university: Columbia, St. Louis, Rolla and Kansas City. The increase was necessary to help cover a $14 million increase in expenses, said University President C. Peter McGrath. Under the new rate schedule, full-time students who are Missouri residents will pay $67.20 a credit hour. They now pay $60 a credit hour. Juniors and seniors will pay $74.30 a credit hour. They now pay $66.30.
Based on a story from the *St. Louis Post-Dispatch.* Used with permission.

4. The oldest subway system in the nation is moving into the 21st century with a plan to replace metal tokens with computerized fare cards, officials said. The Massachusetts Bay Transportation Authority will install an automated fare collection system at a cost of $120 million. The proposed system will offer riders ``smart cards" that passengers wave in front of scanners. Riders will keep their cards and reload them through automated machines, the Internet or the telephone.

5. Researchers have developed a drug that speeds recovery from the common cold. The drug, to be sold by prescription under the brand name Picovir, eases cold symptoms within a day and makes a runny nose completely clear up a day sooner than usual.

9-5. Attribution in leads

Decide whether attribution is or is not needed in the following leads by writing yes or no:

_____ **1.** An employment workshop for foreign students will be at 3:30 p.m. today in the student union.

_____ **2.** Students will receive their enrollment permits in the mail this fall instead of waiting in line for them.

_____ **3.** A fire that caused an estimated $150,000 damage to a home in the western part of the city was caused by a lighted cigarette on a sofa.

_____ **4.** A man shot and killed his wife because he was convinced she was having an affair with his best friend.

_____ **5.** A woman was arrested and charged with hitting a police officer in the face with her key ring.

_____ **6.** A 28-year-old man bashed a relative's car with a baseball bat Saturday night in a dispute over a baseball card.

9-6. Soft leads

Soft leads usually can be classified as descriptive, anecdotal or narrative. Many times a soft lead will have a combination of these qualities. Using some of the leads in your textbook as models, write soft leads as indicated.

1. Write a soft lead, using any technique you wish.

A man in your town was charged yesterday with battery to a law enforcement officer and obstructing official duty. The man was named Harley Dudley Surritte. He was 42 years old and lived at 2313 S.W. Mission Road. He was released on $1,000 bond last night from the county jail. Police said he threw a 2-by-3-foot velvet painting of Elvis Presley off the wall and threw it at officer Chuck Haggard's head. Police said they were sent to Surritte's home at 3:49 p.m. on a report of a domestic fight. Police said Surritte told them he didn't like police officers. "It's the only known Elvis sighting by law enforcement officers in this area," a (your town) police officer said yesterday.
Based on a story from *The Topeka Capital-Journal.* Used with permission.

45

2. Using the focus-on-a-person technique, write an anecdotal lead for this information and include your nut graph.

PHASE is an acronym for Project for Homemakers in Arizona Seeking Employment. It is a program that offers women who have near-poverty level incomes vocational training in largely male-dominated fields such as construction. More than 4,000 single parents and displaced homemakers have received vocational training from the program in the past two years. Tamera Podwolsky used to be a long-distance operator. She answered telephones eight hours a day. She received vocational training through the program. Now she straps on a tool belt and a hard hat and heads for work at local construction sites as a carpentry apprentice. She is 35.

Adapted from a story in *The Arizona Daily Star.*

3. Write a descriptive "show-in-action" lead including the nut graph.

Your community has a home renovation program called Model Block. It is for homeowners who are elderly or disadvantaged and unable to repair their homes. This past weekend 45 people in three neighborhoods in your community were treated to free exterior home remodeling as part of that program. Robert Thompson was one of them. He stood on his newly repaired porch and watched as volunteers, with tools and paintbrushes, scurried around his neighborhood. Thompson and his wife, Flora, were unable to pay for repairs to their home after a van hit the side of their house more than a year ago. Matters became worse when Flora Thompson suffered a stroke that left her paralyzed on her left side. About 400 volunteers took part in the program to give free repairs during the weekend.

Based on a story in *The Topeka Capital-Journal.* Used with permission.

4. Write a narrative lead (reconstructing the event) for the following information:

You are writing an anniversary story about Pearl Harbor, Dec. 7, 1941. On that day, Japanese fighter pilots bombed Pearl Harbor in Hawaii, killing 2,471 Americans and drawing the United States into World War II. The Japanese lost 55 men. You interview a World War II veteran, Earl Schaeffer. On that date he was 19 years old and he was Pvt. Earl Schaeffer. He was stationed at Hickam Field in Oahu, Hawaii.

He tells you what he was doing on Dec. 7, 1941. He says it was a quiet Sunday morning. He was sitting at the switchboard at Hickam Field in Oahu, Hawaii. He says not a single phone call came across the wire. The only sound was the voice on the radio, speaking during the "Lutheran Hour." He says he was studying a book about aerial navigation. He wanted to be a fighter pilot. He began to hear sounds of bombing. It hardly drew his attention. Practice maneuvers were common around the base. But the noise grew louder and louder.

"I ran out of the hangar and I saw aircraft swooping down and dropping black objects, and it still didn't dawn on me, because I wasn't expecting anything like that." Then he saw the large red circles painted on the side of the planes, the symbol of Japanese fighter planes.

Based on a story from *The Salina* (Kan.) *Journal.* Used with permission.

5. Write a mystery teaser lead for this information.

The County Commission in your community voted 2-1 yesterday to pass an ordinance banning ownership of 16 species of animals "not normally domesticated," including tigers, lions, bears, elephants, wolves, primates, alligators and crocodiles. The commission's action was prompted by complaints from neighbors of Delores Sampson. To Sampson, her pet named Marriaha is "like any other kitten." She says Marriaha is always trying to jump up on her lap. But there is one big difference between Marriaha and other 22-month-old cats. Marriaha is a 300-pound Bengal tiger. In December Marriaha escaped from a cage on the back porch and traipsed around her front lawn, separated from her neighbor's yard by just a 4-foot high chain-link fence.

Based on a story from *The* (Louisville , Ky.) *Courier-Journal.* Used with permission.

9-7. Summary and soft leads

This exercise is intended to show you that some stories can have a soft- or hard-news leads. Write a summary lead and then write a soft feature lead for each of these stories:

1. A student at a private school in Vermont disrobed in the middle of her graduation speech. Her name was Kate Logan. She was 18. The school was Long Trail School in Dorset, Vermont. She said she made the decision several months before graduation when she was searching for some way to mark the significance of the event. She stepped to the front of the graduation podium and talked of her journey to a road less traveled. Then she slipped out of her graduation robe and finished her speech naked. School officials were not amused.

2. An unknown boy has been buried for 41 years in a pauper's grave in Philadelphia. His murder has been unsolved. He was known as "the Boy in the Box." Yesterday police exhumed his body in hopes of using modern technology to solve his murder. The medical examiner's office will extract DNA from his remains. Police hope the evidence will help them find the killer. The boy, who was 4 to 6 years old, had been found 41 years ago in a cardboard box. His nude body was covered with dark bruises. He had been wrapped in a flannel blanket. At the time, the medical examiner determined he had been beaten and died from blunt-force trauma.

Based on a story in *The Philadelphia Inquirer* and *Philadelphia Daily News*

3. A growing practice in publishing is making it harder for students to resell their textbooks. The practice is called "bundling," a method of packaging a textbook with supplemental materials such as CD-ROMs. When a book is bundled with a supplement, its ISBN number changes in a database. ISBN stands for International Standard Book Number. Bookstores will only buy back books with ISBNs that match the numbers in a database. Tara Reynold, a senior at a university in the Midwest, is unhappy about that. She says the supplements aren't necessary. "The teachers don't encourage or enforce their use," she says.

Adapted from a story in *The University Daily Kansan*

4. The facts: a Jamaican hotel's plans for Valentine's Day. The hotel is trying to appeal to couples who want to get married. The hotel is offering a nude wedding package for Valentines' Day this year. For $470 a night, the SuperClubs' Hedonism II Resort in Runaway Bay, Jamaica, will provide the minister, the marriage license, the cake and music without charge. You won't need to buy a tuxedo or wedding dress. And you won't need any sunblock.

5. A new study shows that humans can spread germs to their pets. The study shows that cats and dogs can catch bad things from their owners. Canadian researchers documented 16 cases of dangerous, hard to treat staph infections in horses, cats and dogs. They believe that all of them probably began with owners or veterinarians infecting the animals.

9-8. Style quiz

Circle the style errors and correct them in the following sentences.

1. The survey shows that 3 to 4 children die every day from child abuse; more than half of those who died were under age one and seventy-nine% of the deaths were among children under age five.

2. A fire started at 3:00 p.m. and caused 45 thousand dollars worth of damage to a home in the 2,300 block of Main St.

3. Murders in the state are up 53% and violent crime increased two %.

4. A man who threw a two-by-three foot velvet painting of Elvis Presley at officers was 42-years-old.

5. Almost 2500 Americans were killed at Pearl Harbor on December 7, 1941.

6. Tuition will increase twelve % at the University of Missouri and will effect students at all four campuses.

7. 45 people volunteered to repair homes for disadvantaged people.

8. The 36 year old patient said, "I'm going to jump".

9. The two to one vote by the county commission to ban non-domesticated pets will effect Marriaha, a 300 pound Bengal tiger.

10. The tiger lives in a house that has a four-foot fence in the front yard.

Story Structure

10

These exercises will give you a chance to practice endings and different story forms. Check the Web site for this book for other resources: *<http://info.wadsworth.com/rich>*.

10-1. Endings

a. Write a circle kicker (a quote or statement that relates to the lead). The first two paragraphs are the original lead. The remaining information is out of order.

In seventh grade, Christine Arguello read a magazine article about lawyers. The article specifically mentioned Harvard Law School. She decided at that moment she wanted to be a lawyer and she wanted to attend Harvard.

In fact, Harvard was the only law school she applied to after receiving her undergraduate degree in elementary education in 1980 from the University of Colorado.

She practiced law for 11 years in Colorado Springs. Arguello received the 1991 Hispanic of the Year Award in Colorado and was involved in the Colorado Springs community. She often wonders where she would be if she had not read the magazine article about law school.

Being Hispanic was an advantage, Arguello said.

"At times, I had to be twice as good as the next person," she said. "I used it positively and did not dwell on it."

Arguello, who specialized in bankruptcy and commercial litigation, was the first minority to become a partner in the prestigious Denver-based law firm, Holland and Hart. She was also the first Hispanic to be hired by any of the four biggest law firms in Denver.

Based on a story from *The University Daily Kansan.* Used with permission.

b. Write a future kicker; select a paragraph from the story or write your own ending.

Topeka resident Gary Henson may have the largest Batman collection in the world. He hasn't met anybody with more Batman merchandise. His collection contains about 4,000 items. Henson believes Batman's mortality is one reason for his popularity.

Henson, who has owned Quality Carpet Cleaning since 1975, would like to eventually open a Batman museum. He would charge $1 admission only for one reason – so he could buy more Batman merchandise. Henson, 47, has a wide variety of Batman memorabilia, including rare items from the 1960s, such as Batman and Robin bubble bath containers and a Batman lamp.

Based on a story from *The Topeka Capital-Journal.* Used with permission.

10-2. Bright endings

A bright is a brief story with a punchy ending. The emphasis is on the kicker rather than the lead. Brights are often written with a mystery lead to reveal the punch line at the end. They're hard to write, but if you master the technique involved, you'll gain good practice in writing endings. Using the following information, write the full brights – not just the ending. Here is an example of a bright that you may use as a model:

> ### A hairy rescue
> British firefighters managed to rescue a couple and three children from a blazing house in Dudley, England.
>
> But the family was quite concerned about a pet trapped in the inferno.
>
> Firefighters rushed back in.
>
> They found the pet and scooped it up with a soup ladle.
>
> "Thank goodness it was a bit groggy from the smoke, and they were able to put it in a plastic ice-cream container," a fire brigade spokesman said. "We understand it is now recovering."
>
> The pet? A tarantula.
>
> Tom Torok, *The Philadelphia Inquirer*. Reprinted with permission.

a. Write a bright of two paragraphs based on the following information:

A man in your community died last month. After his death, your local County Department of Social Services sent him a letter. The man's name was Albert Maxwell. The man's brother, Jason Maxwell, said the letter is "living proof of how screwed up the system is." The letter said: "Your food stamps will be stopped effective in January because we received a notice that you passed away. You may reapply if there is a change in your circumstances. May God bless you." Rose Josephson, director of the county's social service system, said it's not the fault of her agency. She said the form letter was generated by a computer. She said a caseworker added the "May God bless you," because the employee wanted to soften the message.

b. Write a bright with a factual kicker for this information. Attribute the information to a police report in your town.

Police arrested a 24-year-old man from your town on charges of burglary. The suspect broke into a Domino's pizza parlor on 1700 W. 23rd Street Sunday night. He told police that he had not had anything to eat since Friday night. He said, "I was hungry." It was not known whether the suspect got anything to eat. The man had raided the restaurant cooler. The cooler contained three plastic containers of pizza sauce, 10 pounds of mozzarella cheese and two sacks of flour. A store manager who lives across the street had called the police.

c. Write a bright of five to seven paragraphs with a future kicker:

A little tender loving care was all she wanted

A Colorado Springs male gorilla sensed what a Pittsburgh male gorilla didn't, provided what the Pittsburgh gorilla wouldn't, and now there's a chance he'll be what the Pittsburgh gorilla won't – a daddy.

A 22-year-old female gorilla at the Pittsburgh Zoo had punched one male and ignored two other suitors before the Colorado Springs gorilla came to town in November 1990. Now she has taken to the genteel 27-year-old Westerner, a 400-pound Silverback. He was loaned by the Cheyenne Mountain Zoo in the nationwide Species Survival Plan to breed endangered species in captivity.

"She's going through all the appropriate behavior with him. When she comes into an estrus cycle, she'll come close to him to show that she feels comfortable with him and give him the opportunity to mate," said the zoo's general curator, Lee Nesler.

"She's going to him and eliciting for companionship and whatever comes with that," she said.

"He had been in a social group in the wild and had sired offspring before. He knew how to breed and how to protect the female and the offspring," Nesler said. "We're hoping she can understand this and feel comfortable, and hopefully we'll have a baby gorilla."

Officials at the Pittsburgh Zoo have been watching these hirsute players in the story of love for the past 14 months as they attempted to breed the zoo's first gorilla born in captivity. The gorillas no longer are given names in order to encourage respect for them as wild creatures, zoo officials said.

But wild was not what the Pittsburgh female wanted. Outweighed 2-to-1, she fought off the advances of her former roommate, a 21-year-old, 400-pound Silverback with the aggressive high-strung manners of a bodybuilder on steroids.

"The male from Colorado is very laid-back, very easy-going," Nesler said.

Different females like different types, Nesler said, and they are more likely to conceive and carry their pregnancy to term without aborting when they have chosen their mate. That is why zoos exchange the animals.

Dick Foster, *Rocky Mountain* (Colo.) *News.*
Reprinted with permission.

10-3. Inverted pyramid

Write this story in inverted pyramid order, placing the most newsworthy information first and the rest in descending order of importance. Use a summary lead. You may substitute your town for Portland. Put your quotes in separate paragraphs, unless you have two quotes from the same speaker.

Information from the Portland Fire Bureau: A canister of tear gas was set off by vandals (yesterday morning) at the Gregory Heights Middle School. Three students are being sought for questioning. At least 48 children and two teachers were taken to a dozen Portland hospitals for treatment. The fire department was called at 9:31 a.m. A second alarm was sounded at 10:32 a.m. The problem caused no evacuation of homes in the neighborhood around the school. The school is located at Northeast 73rd Avenue and Siskiyou Street.

Students and teachers vomited and suffered a number of other problems, including a burning sensation in the lungs, nose, throat and eyes, due to the gas that apparently was released in a school corridor. The school was closed for the day. The Fire Bureau began allowing staff members to return inside about noon.

From Don Mayer, spokesman for the Portland Fire Bureau: He said the trips to the hospital were precautionary. He didn't know if anyone was in serious or critical condition. "The symptoms the kids are exhibiting are consistent with Mace." He said a Mace-like container was given to investigators by a parent who said it was sold to her son on the school grounds yesterday morning. Mace is a type of tear gas. He said school officials gave investigators the names of three possible suspects. He said investigators were trying to reach those youths.

From the school Principal John Alkire: He said the substance was in the science and math hall area in the northwest corner of the school's first floor. He said the substance was odorless. "It was like walking into an irritating wall."

From Nguyen Do, an eighth grader: He was in class during the morning break. He said he and others went out in the hall and started coughing. "So I covered my mouth and ran out of the building. It's Mace. I know that. It was a set-up to get out of class or something."

From Michael Grice, spokesman for the Portland Public Schools: Students who were not affected by the fumes were sent home about 10:45 a.m. The school district sent buses to take the students home. Classes at the school will resume tomorrow [use the day of the week].

From Jessie Doty, 12, a seventh-grader: "I started coughing. It just stung my throat. My eyes watered and turned red."

From Jeff MacMillan, 12, a seventh-grader: He said he got a headache from the chemical. He said other classmates were worse off, including one girl who fainted and had to be carried from the building.

From Autumn Gierlich, 13, an eighth-grader who suffers from asthma: She was coughing and receiving oxygen shortly after the incident when you arrived at the school. You notice her waiting for an ambulance and you get these comments from her: "I got the stuff into my lungs, and I could barely breathe. I had to gasp for air. I was dizzy. Now I'm feeling better. They gave me oxygen. I coughed and coughed, and spit up phlegm."

From Richard Harder, a paramedic with the Portland Fire Bureau: He said he was one of the first to arrive. He said he saw about 15 children on the ground. Some of them had severe respiratory problems. Others were coughing, vomiting and sneezing.

From Carol Palumbo, an eighth-grade teacher: She was consoling crying students in front of the school after the evacuation. "The kids are really upset. It's just horrendous, whatever it was."

From your observations and basic questions: Students were taken to an area on the front lawn of the school. They were carried by stretcher or walked to ambulances. The children were ages 12 to 15. More than a dozen ambulances were sent to the school.The school is located at Northeast 73rd Avenue and Siskiyou Street. It has more than 900 staff members and students in the 6th, 7th and 8th grades.

Based on a story by Dave Hogan and Paul Koberstein, *The Oregonian.* Used with permission.

10-4. *The Wall Street Journal* formula

The Wall Street Journal formula uses the concept of specific to general. Stories in this form usually start with an anecdote about a person or description of a particular place or incident and are followed by the nut graph – the main point of the article. It's advisable to place this nut graph high in the story, preferably by the third paragraph. For this exercise, use an anecdotal lead, nut graph and supporting points for this story as discussed in your textbook. You do not have to change the wording in this story; just reorganize the paragraphs in *The Wall Street Journal* formula order. Plan your order topically, and use the kiss-off technique, blocking information from each source.

Voice-mail systems – manufactured by companies such as Octel Communications, AT&T, Rolm and Northern Telecom – basically are one step beyond the household answering machine.

About 85 percent of Fortune 500 firms and 2 million smaller companies are using voice mail, and the $1 billion-a-year voice mail business is still growing 20 percent a year.

Many companies use voice mail as an electronic gatekeeper, routing calls through a main number and an automated attendant. You hear a recording and choose from a menu of departments or services. But it can take a minute or more to go through all the options. This can result in a hefty tab if you happen to be calling long distance. And the 19 percent of U.S. households that still have rotary telephones as opposed to touch-tone phones are really stuck. They can't push buttons to make choices so they're left on hold indefinitely.

Delta Air Lines experimented with voice mail, and some departments – including public relations – discarded it. Says Delta spokesman Bill Berry: "We quickly decided we wanted nothing to do with it. If you call, I don't want you to speak to a mechanical voice."

A company can buy a voice-mail system for $10,000 to $800,000 and can often recoup that investment within 24 hours. Or it can pay the phone company a flat monthly fee for a voice-mail service. Baltimore lawyer Wilbur Jensen, 67, pays C&P Telephone $5 a month and saves the $1,500-a-month cost of a secretary.

"Once you get used to voice mail, it's irreplaceable," says spokesman Bob Powers of the Institute for Electrical and Electronics Engineers.

Melinda Ayala, 40, of Hollywood, Fla., tried to call the Better Business Bureau every day for a week. "I just couldn't get through," says Ayala. "They say, 'Press 2.' You get a busy signal. A recording says, 'Press 5' to be put on hold. You could go on and on with this all day. I don't think it's any way to run a business."

But others argue that nothing can soothe a customer like the human voice. Phyllis Rosen, 48, a receptionist and phone operator at Lyons Financial Group in Charlotte, N.C., says, "I can make or break sales that come into this company by speaking directly to the people that call, by trying to console them. I don't think a machine can do that. It's a very cold way of dealing with people."

NBC-TV tried using voice mail featuring a lengthy electronic menu at its studios in Burbank, Calif. "It was awful," says Rick Romo, West Coast producer of "Today." It infuriated publicists, advertisers and anyone else who called. Two weeks ago NBC dumped it and returned to live operators.

After Karen Malloy, 48, of St. Louis fell down steps recently and wrenched her back, she phoned her doctor. All she got was voice mail – a computerized recording that said the doctor wasn't available.

Because she couldn't get the doctor's OK for an emergency-room visit, her insurer refused to pay the $350 charge.

Her frustration with voice mail, shared by millions daily, reflects a growing disenchantment with the technology.

Complaining about voice mail isn't easy either. Who do you call? The Federal Communications Commission? The Better Business Bureau? Both use voice mail.

Despite its drawbacks, voice mail seems here to stay. As companies downsize to cope with tough economic times, many use voice mail to trim payroll costs or shift operators into other roles.

Hickory Printing Group in Hickory, N.C., has axed voice mail because "customers hated it," says CEO Thomas Reese. His revenue is running 10 percent ahead of the $27 million level a year ago, and he credits the human touch.

Beyond saving money, voice mail makes message taking more accurate because it eliminates human error. . . .

But customers increasingly complain about being stuck on the phone listening to a computerized voice or leaving messages that are never returned. A recent survey by Plog research found that 56 percent of consumers have at some point given up trying to reach a company because of frustrations with voice mail. Those concerns are forcing some companies to rethink or abandon voice-mail technology.

10-5. Hourglass exercise

Write this story in hourglass form, starting with a hard-news lead. Then proceed in chronological order for a portion or the rest of the story. You do not have to use all the information and quotes from the girl in one block. The point of this exercise is to decide when and where you will begin the chronology.

You are making routine calls to the fire department and you receive this report from the dispatcher. Attribute information to fire department officials. Write the story in inverted pyramid order or hourglass form. Use yesterday as your time frame.

Information comes from Neil Heesacker, a spokesman for the fire department in your community. Firefighters responded to a fire at an apartment in a 32-unit apartment complex, Anderson Villa apartments, at 15758 S.E. Division St. at 6:39 a.m. The fire was brought under control at 7:05 a.m. The blaze caused an estimated $50,000 to the apartment building and $10,000 damage to the contents of the apartment. The value of the apartment building is estimated at $480,000. The family's belongings in the apartment that burned were valued at $80,000.

The apartment was rented by Linda Lee Fuson. Her two sons, Kenneth A. J. Fuson, 10, and Michael Fuson, 14, were in the apartment at the time of the fire. Linda Fuson was not. She arrived some time after 6:40 a.m. Her whereabouts before then are unknown. The fire burned through the floor and blistered the gypsum walls and melted the family's television set. Three pet birds died.

The fire also caused smoke damage to the apartment of Pat and Lisa Hampton, who live across the stairs from the Fuson family. The cause of the fire is under investigation. A neighbor, Darren Nitz, 31, is credited with saving Michael Fuson's life. He lives on the first floor, just below the Fusons' apartment. Michael Fuson suffered burns over a third of his body. He is in critical condition at Emanuel Hospital and Health Center's burn unit. He has second- and third-degree burns on his hands, arms, face, neck, back, buttocks and thighs. Kenneth Fuson was trapped in his bedroom. He died in the fire. Fire in an enclosed area such as an apartment can push temperatures to 1,700 degrees Fahrenheit near the ceiling and 1,000 degrees on the floor.

Information from interview with Darren Nitz: "About 6:35 a.m. I heard neighbors pounding on my door and yelling about the fire. I didn't think much about it at first, until someone said two children were trapped in the apartment. Michael was about seven feet from his bedroom door. He was saying 'I can't, I can't,' and rolling over and over. I said, 'We've got to get out of here.' I tried to grab hold of his arm but couldn't because he was so badly burned. I put him over my shoulder and carried him outside. He told me that Kenneth was still upstairs. I went back to the top of the stairs but the flames reached the front door. Another neighbor, Brad Lindsey, grabbed a fire extinguisher and followed me."

From Brad Lindsey, 24. "It was fully going when we got up there. Just after we got up them, it just vacuumed and shot right across the stairway. Nitz and I went back down the stairs. There was no way either of us could do anything about it.

10-6. List technique

Lists are often used to clarify bureaucratic stories, especially those containing numbers. Write this story using the list technique. Your story will be accompanied by a chart.

The U.S. Census Bureau released a report today based on a study the bureau conducted last year. The study was a survey of 23,000 households. It was called "What It's Worth." The study revealed that if you get a college degree, your income will increase by about $1,000 a month.

The study said any post-high school degree, whether it is a trade school certificate or a professional degree, will increase earning power. The study said that more adults than ever – 25.2 percent – now have a post-high school degree. The author of the study, Rebecca Sutterlin, said that's up 20.7 percent from 1984. But the study showed some racial disparities as well as other differences.

People with post-high school degrees earned an average of $2,231 monthly, compared with $1,280 for those with some college but no degree. People with just a high school diploma earned $1,077 a month and those who don't have a high school education averaged $492 a month.

In engineering, 15 percent of men had degrees but only 2 percent of women.

The average monthly earnings for professionals were $4,961. People with a doctorate averaged $3,855 a month. People with a master's degree averaged $2,822 a month and those with a bachelor's degree averaged $2,116 a month.

On the average, blacks earn significantly less than whites at each educational level, with the exception of blacks with master's degrees. Blacks with bachelor's degrees earned an average of $1,814 a month, compared to $2,149 for whites.

Of the adults over 18 who hadn't finished high school, 19.4 percent were white, compared with 31.9 percent of blacks and 43.8 percent of Hispanics. For college degrees, 26.4 percent of whites have college degrees, compared to 14 percent of blacks and 11.6 percent of Hispanics.

Based on a story from *USA Today*. Copyright 1993. Used with permission.

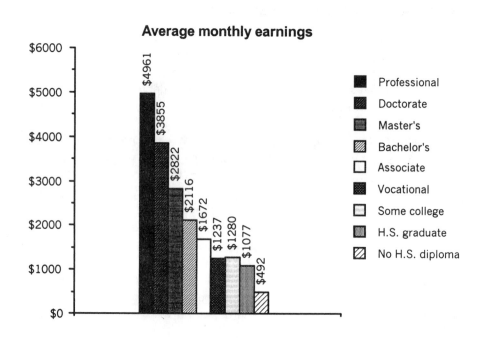

Average monthly earnings

■	Professional
▨	Doctorate
▤	Master's
▨	Bachelor's
□	Associate
▦	Vocational
▢	Some college
▥	H.S. graduate
▨	No H.S. diploma

10-7. Style test

Correct the errors in the following sentences:

1. The government estimates that more than 11,000 sea turtles drown in shrimp nets in waters in the U.S. each year.

2. A shrimper was imprisoned for failing to use a federally-mandated turtle protection device on his boat.

3. The store was at 1,202 Maple Rd.

4. There were 10 lbs. of cheese and four lbs. of tomatoes in the refrigerator.

5. Houston Police Sergeant Roy House said the suspect defrauded employers out of $150,000 dollars.

6. The United States Department of Agriculture (first reference) employs 7,000 meat inspectors.

7. The USDA (second reference) operates a training center at College Station, Texas where veterinarians attended classes.

8. The defendent was convicted of possessing three ounces of cocaine.

9. The story was about a woman with Alzheimers Disease.

10. The female gorilla is from the east coast.

Storytelling and Feature Techniques

11

This chapter will help you develop ways to make your writing more colorful by using descriptive and narrative writing techniques. Check into the Web site for this book for more storytelling resources and links to sites mentioned here:

<http://info.wadsworth.com/rich>.

11-1. Storytelling mindset exercises

a. Fiction to fact: Take any fiction short story that you like and write it in newspaper style using storytelling techniques. Short stories by Edgar Allan Poe could work well in this exercise. Check the Poe museum at *www.poemuseum.org*.

b. Fact like fiction: Using storytelling techniques but sticking to the facts, turn a story from the *National Enquirer* or any other supermarket tabloid into a newspaper story *www.nationalenquirer.com*.

c. Fun facts: Take a basic news story from your campus or local newspaper and write it in the style of a supermarket tabloid newspaper.

11-2. Storytelling for a crime story

Write this story using narrative writing style. Here are your notes:

It is the Christmas season. A woman was shopping at the Galleria shopping mall in Fort Lauderdale. A man robbed the woman after she got into her unlocked car. The suspect has not been caught. Police described him as a white man about 27 years old, 5 feet 7 inches tall, with brown hair and brown eyes. He was described as clean-shaven but unkempt. He stole her wallet.

You interview the woman who was robbed. Her name is Pauline Cayia and she lives in Fort Lauderdale. She said she finished shopping about 7 p.m. Sunday and returned to her unlocked car at the Galleria mall. She said she had been shopping for about an hour and a half. She manages a recording studio.

She said the robber was polite and well spoken. She said he took her wallet, but on Monday (a few hours before you interview her) she received a phone call that her wallet had been found. It was returned along with her credit cards and driver's license. Only her $85 in cash was missing.

She said as she got into her car, she smelled a strong body odor. She drove away from the shopping center at 2700 E. Sunrise Blvd. and a man popped up in the back seat and demanded her purse. She said the robber went through her purse as she was driving south along Federal Highway toward Broward Boulevard.

"Before I got in the car, I looked around and didn't see anything. I smelled an odor when I put my packages in the front seat, and I checked the back seat, but I didn't see anybody. I suppose he was sleeping, because he didn't say anything until I got to Federal Highway. He said, 'Ma'am, give me your purse and let me off here.' I started going fast to try to attract the attention of a policeman, but I didn't find anybody to stop me. I was going fast, and he said, 'You're going to kill us.'"

When she was driving toward Broward Boulevard, the robber returned her purse. "He said, 'Here's your purse' and threw it into the front seat, but he kept my wallet."

At Federal and Broward, Cayia slowed to turn and ended up hitting a car. At that point, the robber jumped out and ran, even though the car was still moving. She drove directly to the police station. "I don't know if I was scared or in control. I just wanted to get the police."

Based on a story from the *Sun-Sentinel* (Fort Lauderdale, Fla.). Used with permission.

11-3. Storytelling news feature

This storytelling exercise was devised by Alan Richman, former writer and writing coach for *The Boston Globe* and now a writer for *GQ (Gentleman's Quarterly)*. Richman wrote this story when he was at *The Globe*. His assignment was to follow up on a news story with a feature. The news story is reprinted here; then you will get Richman's notes. Use those notes to write a feature in no more than 750 words – about 16 inches in a newspaper story. The point of the exercise is to see how many details and rich quotes you can fit in that amount of space. As you read Richman's notes, consider how much detail he gathered. You will also have to decide if you should use anonymous sources.

> An East Boston man confessed to stealing a car last Thursday and spending most of the $10,000 in cash he found in the glove compartment before he was caught on Saturday, police said.
>
> Michael Yanelli, 22, of 569 Bennington St., East Boston, was arrested at 9:15 Saturday night and charged with stealing a 1979 Cadillac belonging to Rene Gignac of Laconia, N.H.
>
> The car, which had been discovered missing at 11:45 a.m. Thursday, had been parked in front of 880 Saratoga St., East Boston. Police said that besides a briefcase, papers and wallet on the seat of the car, the glove compartment contained $30,000 in checks and $10,000 in cash.
>
> Yanelli's arrest came after a police investigation and tips from neighborhood contacts. A police spokesman said Yanelli admitted to the theft in a deposition and said he had spent most of the money he found. He turned over $2,682 in cash and $1,972 worth of plane tickets, the spokesman said.
>
> Yanelli was charged with larceny over $100, and will be arraigned in East Boston District Court tomorrow morning, police said.

•   •   •

Three days after this story appears, an editor decides that it should be followed up. The editor wants to know: Who is this guy? How did he manage to spend more than $7,000 in less than two days? How does he feel about his windfall?

You are assigned to write the follow-up story. All you know, in addition to what you read in the brief news story, is that Boston has the highest car theft rate in the United States and East Boston, one of the neighborhoods within the city, has the highest car theft rate in Boston. It's a lower-middle class, blue collar neighborhood.

You go out to report your story. This is what you find out:

Yanelli lives on a tree-lined residential street not far from Wonderland, a greyhound race track. A church, St. Mary's Star of the Sea, is across the street from his home. In the same building, below his apartment, is Carlo's Cold Cut Centre, a tiny neighborhood grocery. The building he lives in is a little seedy, with a broken window, ugly asphalt shingle sidings, no names on the mailboxes.

You talk to a teen-age girl with deep lavender eye shadow. She is walking down the street. She won't give her name. She knows Yanelli, says he's a little slow. She says, "If I found $10,000, I wouldn't tell anyone. I'd get right out of the car."

You go to 880 Saratoga St., which is four blocks from his apartment. It's one address in a series of garden apartments called "Brandywine Village." You stop three elderly ladies walking down the street. They won't give their names, but they tell you that Gignac was helping his mother-in-law move and the money in the glove compartment was for a down payment on a new house or condominium for her.

"The daughter told me that," the first lady says.

"I wouldn't leave that money in a car," says the second. "I'd put it in my bloomers."

You go to the local police precinct, District Seven. They know Yanelli by reputation.

"He's a little addle-brained," one cop tells you.

The crime report is down at District 1, police headquarters. You call and find out that Yanelli is charged with larceny of a motor vehicle worth more than $9,000, stealing $10,060 in U.S. currency, stealing three credit cards and three checks. He pleaded not guilty and was sent to Charles Street Jail, the city jail. He did not post bail. His court attorney is Paul Luciano. You call him but he is out of town.

The detective investigating the case tells you, off the record, that Yanelli destroyed the checks, kept the cash and bought two first-class airline tickets to Las Vegas for $1,800. He kept the money in a brown paper bag. He changed plates on the car. The tips came when he was seen flashing a lot of money around the neighborhood.

At the East District Court, people tell you that Yanelli is a big kid with a shaved head, a little slow.

You find it interesting that everyone you speak to tells you how dumb Yanelli was to keep the car. Everybody – even the policemen – says that he should have ditched the car as soon as he found the cash.

You try to call Rene Gignac in New Hampshire. He has an unlisted number.

The Charles Street Jail is run by the Suffolk County sheriff. You call and ask to speak to Yanelli. A public relations official for the sheriff's department says she will make the request. She says she will also advise Yanelli to talk to his lawyer before talking to you. You get lucky. Yanelli tries for more than a day, but his lawyer is still out of town. He says he'll talk to you. The following are your quotes from the interview:

You: What did you feel when you saw the money?

Him: My heart went 90 miles an hour.

You: Describe what the money looked like.

Him: It was about this big. (He makes a 4-inch space with his hands.) It was 100s, 50s, 10s. The glove compartment was open. There was a briefcase in the front seat with $60 in it.

You: Why did you steal the car in the first place?

Him: A joyride. Just to take the car. It's a habit with me. It ain't going to happen anymore.

You: What did you think after you got in the car and were riding around?

Him: This guy (Gignac) is so stupid. I got to talk to the guy. I've only been charged with larceny of a motor vehicle. I wasn't charged with stealing money. If I have to do any time, I want them to prove it. I have three previous larcenies of motor vehicles – all the cars had keys in them. One in Malden, one in East Boston, one in Winthrop. This is the fourth.

Him continued: I drove away and noticed the car was on empty, so I went for gas. I opened the briefcase. There was $60 in it. I put $20 in and got half a tank. I opened the glove compartment, looking for something to blow my nose. I threw out a white envelope. 20s and 50s and 100s piled out.

You: What did you spend it on?

Him: I was going to Vegas the next day. Thursday afternoon I had the money. I bought a couple of things, a color television for my best friend because he was getting married. I went out and bought $600 worth of clothes, paid back a couple of debts. The two airline tickets to Vegas cost $1,972. I was going to go, but didn't. I was going to take a friend but he said he wanted to stay home for the 4th of July. My brother said to me, "Get rid of the car." Yeah, I know, I know. Why didn't I? I almost did. I even drove to Revere (a small city adjoining Boston) on Thursday to Cerretani's parking lot (a grocery store), wiped my fingerprints off the car. I was throwing the keys away. I hesitated. I said no. I needed a couple more things. I went to lunch. I took a cab home. I went to the dog track, lost a couple hundred. Thursday night I went to Jeveli's (a restaurant) in East Boston and ate. I went home. Friday morning a friend of mine picked up the briefcase. He gets rid of the briefcase. This guy (Gignac) is completely stupid – there's $60,000 - $70,000 in money orders in the briefcase. The checkbook shows 80,000 bucks. I'm down on this guy. It's his fault. Friday morning I went back to get the car. A friend and I went to Suffolk Downs (a thoroughbred racing track in East Boston). I end up winning $1,500. I had the perfecta in the last race.

(The perfecta is a type of bet based on winning first and second place finishers. Note: You check the race results. In the 10th at Suffolk Downs, Fleet Concessioner, an 8-1 shot, finished first and Marshua's Romeo finished second. The perfecta paid $115 for a $2 bet.)

Him: I said to my friend, "I'll go get my mother and father a color TV. A Sears TV." My mother turned it back. She wouldn't take it. I spent $1,700 on a TV for a friend's mother and father, a Sony Trinitron. I gave the store $50 to have it delivered. Friday night another friend and I went out to the Kowloon (a glittery Polynesian restaurant). We were there from 8 until 11:30. We had four pu-pu platters. We ditched the car in Lynn (another city) and went home. They never would have found it; I hid it so good. On Saturday, Tommy and Jimmy, two cops who arrested me before, came to my house. They told me I might as well admit it. They're good cops. I gave them the rest of the money. I told them where the car was.

(He thinks that Gignac saw him in the car and picked him out from a mug book.)

Him: I know all the guards. They like me. (He has been in Charles Street Jail before.)

I got to learn my lesson sooner or later. I got to serve time so I don't do this anymore. And tell people to leave their cars locked up and don't leave $10,000 in the car where anybody can get it. He left his wallet in the car, too. This guy is a complete idiot.

(He tells you he's 22, unemployed, living in East Boston practically his whole life, graduated from Boston Technical High School in 1978 and is well liked around the neighborhood.)

Him: I can't hold on to a job. I got a temper and a half.

You: Did you have a good time?

Him: Yeah. It was great. I love flashing 100s around. I spent it on true friends, though.

You: What else did you buy?

Him: Watch, clothes, ring, radio, 4 Beatles tapes. If I do time, I want to do it here (Charles Street Jail). I like it here.

He is dressed in a T-shirt, Army fatigue pants and basketball shoes. He says he also bought four pairs of basketball shoes.

The editor tells you to write it in 750 words.

Public Relations Writing   12

The following exercises will give you a chance to do some critical thinking about news releases, media kits and chances to create your own public relations materials. Check the Web site for this book for online resources that offer many helpful hints on writing press releases and media kits: *http://info.wadsworth.com/rich*

12-1. Qualities of news releases

 Write the answers in your computer, and print out the page.

1. List three qualities of news that your press releases should have for print publications.

2. List three qualities of news that your press releases should have for broadcast (TV).

3. List crucial contact information that all press releases should contain.

4. List any additional qualities that your Web site press releases should contain. How would a Web press release differ from print releases?

5. How would a press release for print differ from one sent by e-mail?

6. Make a template (a form) for a print press release. Use the form in your textbook as a guide.

7. Make a template for a fax press release.

8. Compare news releases on three university Web sites. You can and should check your own college Web site if you have one. If not, choose your favorite colleges or universities and check out their Web news releases. You can link to them from Yahoo! *www.yahoo.com* and search for college and universities or
http://dir.yahoo.com/Education/Higher_Education/Colleges_and_Universities/.

9. Discussion:

 • How do they differ?

 • Which do you like?

 • Which are most helpful?

 • Which would you use if you were an editor at a newspaper?

 • Which would you use if you were a news director at a TV station?

 • How do they differ from a news or feature story you have been taught to write?

10. Now study a corporate public relations wire service. Click into:

www.prnewswire.com or www.businesswire.com

Study a feature package.

Study a news release from a corporation.

Discuss the differences.

12-2. Gather information and write news releases

Check information from bulletin boards in your school. Gather information for three events for which you will write press releases.

1. Write one version for print via mail and fax.

2. Write another version for broadcast.

3. Write another version for the Web.

4. Write another version for e-mail.

12-3. Rewrite a news release

This news release about an event is poorly written and is not in proper form. It also has style errors. Rewrite this release using proper form (name of organization, address, your name as contact and your telephone number and e-mail address); date the release, write a headline and write "FOR IMMEDIATE RELEASE" on the left or above the headline. Double-space the release and type – 30 – at the end. Write one or two paragraphs and eliminate extraneous information.

News Release

To whom it may concern:

Big Brothers/Big Sisters of Douglas County, Inc. will host an informational meeting for prospective volunteers at 10:00 a.m., Saturday, (add Saturday's date). We would be so happy to have you attend, and we would welcome news coverage. The meeting will be at the organization's office at 220 Main st. in Lawrence, 04040. The meeting will last approximately 2 hours and officers of Big Brothers/Big Sisters will discuss how you can become a volunteer to a child who needs adult companionship, which is the purpose of the organization. If you would like more information, call 454-1222 anytime during the week. We are hoping to gain more volunteers for the organization, and will appreciate anything you can do to help us.

 I am George Hand, contact for the organization, and I would be happy to talk with you about it. You can call me at the organization's office, 454-1222.

P.S. If anyone can't make this meeting, another informational meeting is scheduled for Tuesday, [add Tuesday's date]. That will be at 6:00 p.m.

12-4. News release

Assume this is a news release issued by the Office of University Relations at your university, which has a total enrollment of 24,500 students. Use a hard-news lead and write it in inverted pyramid style. Limit it to one page. Write a headline and use standard press release form. Label it "NEWS RELEASE" and put the University and contact information at the top; use your phone number and e-mail address. You may use today's date and "FOR IMMEDIATE RELEASE." Consider a chart or list format for some of the statistics. Here is the information, which is poorly written.

The university has released figures for its minority enrollment for this fall. The enrollment categories are based on self-reported student data. The minority enrollment has increased. In fact, it increased 8.7 percent this fall. This increase came in a year when overall campus enrollment grew less than 1 percent.

"This university has taken a significant step forward," said [Use the name of your university president or chancellor]. "Our many efforts of recent years are beginning to produce the desired results."

Enrollment of black students increased by 34 students to 678.

"The increase in minority students is a gratifying sight for the many students, faculty and administrators who have worked for it," the chancellor (use his or her name) said. "We still have more to do. This is only the beginning."

In other categories, American Indian student enrollment showed the largest increase of 46 students to a total of 204. Asian student enrollment increased by 44 to 565. Hispanic enrollment grew by 28 to 452.

Comparing minority enrollment for previous years, the statistics show that minority enrollment for five years ago was 1,540 compared to 1,747 last year and 1,899 this year.

Based on a press release from the Office of University Relations, University of Kansas. Used with permission.

12-5. News feature release

You are working for the Office of University Relations for your university. A professor of anthropology has written a book about the hidden consequences of tests. You are writing a feature press release that you hope will be reprinted in newspapers throughout your state. Label this "NEWS RELEASE." Include contacts, your phone number, date of the release and "FOR IMMEDIATE RELEASE." Write a headline, as well, and double space your copy. If you use a soft lead, make sure you get to the point very quickly, preferably in the second paragraph. First write a brief that can be used as a teaser in a "News Tips" release to accompany this release. Then write the full release, which can be one to two pages.

F. Allan Hanson, professor of anthropology at the University of (insert your college or university name), has written a book. The book, "Testing Testing: Social Consequences of the Examined Life," is published by University of California Press and is available at local bookstores or by contacting Denise Cicourel at UC Press, 2120 Berkeley Way, Berkeley, CA 94720.

The book is about American society's addiction to tests. Hanson uncovers a variety of hidden consequences – many of them unsavory – of tests commonly used in business and education. He recommends eliminating most drug tests, intelligence and aptitude tests, and lie detector or integrity tests.

Employers use drug testing and integrity testing to screen applicants and monitor employees.

Hanson recommends eliminating integrity testing and using drug tests only when people are suspected of using drugs.

An exception is testing for anabolic steroids. Because the effects of steroids remain long after the drug can be detected by tests, Hanson says, "random testing is about the only way we can discover the use of the drug in athletic competition."

"The American preoccupation with testing has resulted in a panoply of techniques dedicated to scanning, probing, weighing, perusing and recording every last detail of our personal traits and life experiences," Hanson says.

Hanson says it should be possible to eliminate much of the testing used to predict behavior and aptitudes. For example, some college admissions offices no longer require scores from aptitude tests such as the American College Test, or ACT, or Scholastic Aptitude Test, or GMAT, as an application requirement.

Of all forms of testing, Hanson finds lie detectors the vilest, a pornographic gaze into a person's private thoughts. The test taker is powerless to conceal or control anything, and the test results are often unreliable, he says. Yet people whose character may be under public scrutiny submit to and even request polygraph tests to establish credibility.

The future is likely to produce even more detailed knowledge of each individual as new genetic tests and DNA fingerprinting are developed, he says.

Hanson says tests that measure performance, such as what a student has learned in class or skills mastered for a job, are useful.

But tests that predict behavior or aptitude – IQ tests, for example – can have unintended and undesirable consequences, he argues. Scores from IQ tests can become life sentences for children with very high or very low scores. Tests assign people to various categories – genius, slow learner, security risk – "Where they are then treated, act and come to think of themselves according to the expectations associated with those categories," Hanson says.

"People are examined and evaluated less for qualifications or knowledge they already possess than for what the test results can predict about future actions or potential behavior," Hanson says.

"Decisions are made about people not on the basis of what they have done, or even what they certainly will do, but in terms of what they might do."

Because tests provide information about people, they serve as devices of power for agencies – employers, educational administrators, insurance firms, law enforcement agencies – to determine whom to employ, to admit to college, to take on as a risk or to arrest.

Based on a press release from the Office of University Relations, University of Kansas. Used with permission.

12-6. Web news release

Using the following information, write a news release for the Web. Instead of double-spacing, as in print releases, use single spacing, and insert a space between paragraphs. Be sure to include relevant URLs for the company. You may use a hard-news or feature approach. Limit your release to no more than two screens, preferably one screen. Put a posting date at the end of your document. Use proper AP style. (You might want to check out the site before you write your release.)

Headline: This is about offering free greeting cards with astrological messages
Press Contact: You (and your phone numbers and e-mail address)
The company name is Access: NewAge. The Web site address is
http://www.accessnewage.com.

Here is the information: The company prides itself on being a major link to the spiritual and New Age community. Access: NewAge is expanding its services by offering free online personalized astrological greeting cards. For example: Happy Birthday, Sagittarian . . . or Libra . . . or Gemini. Or possibly Congratulations Pisces. I love you Taurus. Good luck Leo. These are some examples.

You can now send friends, lovers, and family free astrological greeting cards courtesy of Access: NewAge.

Our Web site address is *http://www.accessnewage.com.*

Each card contains an astrological profile and a link to an up-to-date monthly horoscope for the sign. Senders can send their greeting with any message and choose a special background. If they know HTML, they can code the greeting card effects.

Bob Siegel, webmaster of the company's Web site (www.accessewAge.com) says, "Access: NewAge was created with the intent of offering content on all things esoteric, spiritual and metaphysical. Free customizable astrological greeting cards are the step. And, if visitors want to order a gift to go with the card, like a book or aromatherapy products, they can do that at our site."

The Web site, *www.accessnewage.com* was launched in 1995 and currently boasts over 30,000 unique visitors a day and provides links to other esoteric, spiritual and new age sites. The site's Looking Deeper Magazine offers visitors hundreds of online articles from some of the top new age specialists in the field and forecasts from our resident astrologer.

Company Name: Access: NewAge
Web address: *http://www.accessnewage.com*
Posted: Today's date.

12-7. Product promotion - print and Web

Write this news release in print form. Then convert it to Web format. Your textbook contains a press release from Binney & Smith to promote Crayola new washable crayons. Now the company has come out with another new product – its first highlighters for kids. They, too, are washable. Write a press release to promote this product. Use standard double-space form, and limit your release to one page (approximately three to four paragraphs). Make sure you include the company name, address, telephone number, and use your name as the contact person with your telephone number. Label your release "For Immediate Release." Write a headline at the top of the release, and use Easton, Pa. as your dateline. Here is the information:

The company uses "From Crayola Products" above its name, Binney & Smith, Inc., 1100 Church Lane, P.O. Box 431, Easton, Pennsylvania 18044-0431 [use your phone number].

Binney & Smith is the maker of Crayola products, which include crayons and markers and paints and a variety of other products. The company is introducing a new line of products, which it says is its first set of highlighters specifically designed for kids.

The product will be called Crayola Screamin' Neons. These are washable school highlighters that were designed especially for schoolchildren. The products are bright, neon colors. Bright, neon graphics on each highlighter "scream" kids and fun. The highlighters feature a special rounded nib that allows a smooth flow of ink without noise or squeaking. They are washable. The washable formula is patented. It allows the highlighter ink to be washed from hands, face and most children's clothing. They are non-toxic. They are available in a pack of four colors: glowing green, neon yellow, hot magenta and electric blue.

The suggested retail price is $1.99. The highlighters were developed after research conducted by Binney & Smith revealed that children start using highlighters around the age of 8. The research also revealed that they continue using highlighters throughout their school use. The research also indicated that children use highlighters for a variety of activities. Some of those activities include school papers, study sheets, plays, maps and reports. Tailoring a highlighter to the needs of children resulted in the development of Screamin' Neons.

In addition to the press release information for this product, you are including this background about the company; decide if any of this should go in the press release or should be packaged separately:

Binney & Smith, maker of Crayola Products, was founded by C. Harold Smith and Edwin Binney in 1885. Slate pencils and chalk preceded the company's introduction of Crayola crayons in 1903.

Each year Binney & Smith produces more than 2 billion Crayola crayons.

Tests reveal that the smell of Crayola crayons is one of the 20 most recognizable aromas to American adults. Coffee and peanut butter top the list.

On the average, children ages 2 to 7 color or draw 28 minutes a day.

In a given year, Binney & Smith manufactures enough Crayola paint to cover all of the major league baseball and football stadiums and the Brooklyn Bridge combined.

In addition to crayons, Crayola products include markers, watercolors, tempera paints, chalk, clay, washable paints as well as fabric paints.

Each year American children spent 6.3 billion hours coloring – almost 10,000 human lifetimes.

Crayola crayons are currently sold in more than 60 countries from the island of Iceland to the tiny Central American nation of Belize. Crayola product boxes are printed in 11 different languages including English, Spanish, French, Dutch and Italian.

The first box of Crayola crayons sold for 5 cents.

Based on a news release from Binney & Smith. Used with permission.

12-8. Interviews for news release format

Interview members of the local print and broadcast media: section editors or news directors. Ask how they prefer to receive press releases: print, fax or e-mail? Ask what kind of news they are interested in receiving. If you do this as a class exercise in groups, decide who will call whom so you aren't calling the same people.

12-9. Design a media kit

Choose an organization or topic (upcoming holiday). A local nonprofit organization would be a good client. Design a media kit that includes:
- Press releases about upcoming news.
- Backgrounder about the organization or company.
- Feature story about the organization or company.
- Photos or graphics (or suggestions for either).
- Related Web links for the organization.
- Cover (optional) with creative graphic.

Suggestions for study: Click into a Web site for a major company or organization.

Hallmark: *www.hallmark.com*

Any nonprofit organization.

12-10. Creative preview publicity planning

Barbara Brown is a highly successful public relations practitioner in Anchorage, Alaska. As a publicity director for the Municipality of Anchorage, she takes an unconventional approach to publicizing events the library and other city agencies want to promote. Her advice is to consider the following:

- Do you want before-the-event news so people will come (fund raiser) or after-the-event news so results are reported?
- TV is a visual medium; to get before-the-event news, you may need to create a special media event such as a special preview option.

For example, to publicize the 10th anniversary of the Anchorage Loussac Library, she created a media event. She planned a giant birthday cake, a scale model of the library, to feed 400 people. Then she invited the media to come before the event and get video of the people making the cake. Her news release was equally unconventional. It featured this headline:

It's a
Giant
Birthday Cake

Now it's your turn. How would you find a creative way to publicize the following information?

Your city's parks and recreation department is taking its annual check of the outdoor ice-skating rinks to determine if the ice is thick enough to be safe. The fire department will be digging into the ice and taking samples to check if it is at least 12 inches thick. When the ice is thick enough, the lakes will be opened for ice hockey and ice skating. All lakes will remain closed until the ice is at least 12 inches thick. The fire department will take its first samples on Thursday, (use this week's date), at 10:30 a.m. Use a location in your community. What creative, visual approach could you take to get the media, particularly TV, to cover this event? Write a news release incorporating your approach. Use a creative headline.

Broadcast Writing

13

This chapter will give you some practice writing basic broadcast stories for the anchors to read (on camera readers) and for a reporter package. For the following exercises, assume you are working in a large- to medium-sized market. These stories are interesting, but they're not the most important stories in tonight's newscast, so you must keep them tight by focusing on the important and interesting elements that your audience will want to know. Other exercises are designed to sharpen your skills in word choice and leads. Check the Web site for this book for links to broadcast resources: *http://info.wadsworth.com/rich.*

13-1. Church embezzler

Write a television news story from the following notes. First decide the focus of the story. Then write a lead, either direct or indirect, related to your focus. Write the story as a :20 (20 second) anchor on-camera reader, a story with no video, only the anchor reading on camera. Assume that these locations are in your community or substitute with your cities or towns. Use correct style for broadcast.

A trial has just ended in Johnson County District Court. The defendant, Ron Poteet, 26, 1010 Wellington Road, was caught pocketing monies from the collection plate at Presbyterian Fellowship Church, 2416 Clinton Parkway. Both addresses are in Overland Park (or your city). He was arrested on June 6 of the previous year. He had been entrusted with counting the daily donations and was sentenced earlier today (just after 2 p.m.) to three years in prison. That was his job since 1996.

The pastor of the church, Gordon Price, said yesterday that he had been impressed from the beginning with Poteet's work and thought he was "extremely nice. Polite. Reserved. Gentlehearted. I assumed everything was OK. I was wrong."

Poteet was caught when discrepancies between the amounts entered on the donation envelopes, and the actual amount of money contained inside the envelopes were noticed by another church employee. The investigation was then handed over to the police. In all, about $70,000 was taken by Poteet, although the exact amount isn't known. Price said he debated a long time over whether or not to prosecute.

Poteet was sentenced in courtroom D by Judge Jane Shepherdson to serve 3 years and pay a fine of $10,000. He had pleaded guilty earlier. He made no statement to the court, either when he pleaded or was sentenced.

Exercise written by John Broholm, broadcast journalism professor at the University of Kansas.

71

13-2. Lumber fire

Write a brief "voiceover" story, a story with accompanying videotape, for this follow-up story. Follow-up stories run a day or more after the event covered to update viewers on recent developments. Your story will run on your station's 6:00 evening newscast. The fire happened in a small, nearby community, which received aid from the fire department at another nearby community. Your station was able to obtain videotape of the fire but no interviews from the scene, and your information comes from a wire story. The first sentence of your story will be "on camera," and then the director will go to the videotape.

(DELTON) – Investigators continued to search for the cause of a fire last night that heavily damaged the Delton Lumber Co., while the lumber company's owner worked to get back into business.

The blaze was fought by firefighters from Springfield and Delton as part of a mutual aid pact signed by the two cities.

A 4 p.m. meeting was scheduled for today by fire and law enforcement officials from Springfield and Delton at the Springfield/Hamilton County Law Enforcement Center to discuss the fire that destroyed two buildings at the lumberyard and a nearby historic railroad depot, which was used for storage by the lumber company.

No one was injured in the fire that began at approximately 8:30 p.m. in one of the lumber yard buildings, spread to the depot and burned brightly in the night sky until it was brought under control at about 11:00 p.m.

"We're just going to discuss the investigation and where we need to go from here," Springfield Fire Chief Herman McMahon said today.

McMahon said he, Hamilton County Sheriff John Chavez, Delton's acting police chief, Kenny Gault, and Larry Westerman, a Springfield firefighter in charge of the investigation, would be among officials at the meeting.

Dennis Salyer, lumberyard owner, said he hoped to be doing business in a limited way within one or two days, depending on how much the fire episode had disrupted power and lights to the lumberyard office, which suffered only smoke damage.

"We'll do the best we can because we've got some contractor customers who need lumber for building projects," said Salyer.

Officials haven't determined the cause of the fire, which resulted in at least $200,000 in damage.

An official estimate of the damage is being withheld pending inspection by insurance adjusters, McMahon said.

Exercise written by John Broholm, broadcast journalism professor at the University of Kansas.

13-3. Acid arrests

From the following notes, write a short package news story, with an anchor intro and with your recorded voice delivering the main section of the story. Use one or two sound bites with news sources from the quoted material in the notes. You may substitute the names of your community for the ones in this story.

You have been told by Otto Privette, the regional director of the Drug Enforcement Administration, the arm of the U.S. Justice Department that is concerned with illegal drug trafficking, that the D.E.A., the F.B.I., and local law enforcement agencies in northeastern Kansas have seen a significant hike in arrests for sale and/or use of LSD. All told, there have been 10 arrests since the beginning of the year, up from just three all of last year, according to Privette, and the year still has four months to go. LSD was a popular hallucinogenic, countercultural drug in the 1960s. (Phone calls to local law enforcement offices confirmed Privette's assertion of an increase in arrests.) Privette predicted 10 more arrests during the remainder of the year.

Privette said that overall in the Kansas City and Lawrence areas:

"More people are using acid, and we're sure arresting more people these days. It's a good bet we'll make some more arrests because we've got three investigators running down leads full-time. In a way it's discouraging because there's so much of the drug around, but I think we're making some headway on the problem." (:12)

Privette said police in the region were looking to arrest manufacturers, sellers, and users, and they're particularly on the lookout for clues leading to the apprehension of a probable local manufacturer of the drug. Privette said it was common for LSD to be manufactured locally.

Lynne Harris, who works for the state of Kansas as a counselor for juveniles who have been arrested on drug-related offenses, said police were arresting many teenagers on LSD-related offenses. She said the drug was popular with teenagers because it was relatively inexpensive and provided a longer "trip" or high than many other drugs. LSD manufacturers have always added one of many varieties of stimulant to the drug to accelerate its entry into and assimilation by the human metabolism, according to Harris. She said the intended purpose of the stimulant was to enhance the sensation of euphoria, or "rush," caused by the drug. She said she didn't know whether the strychnine contamination was for that purpose, or was simply a byproduct of drug production:

"A lot of the LSD we've been seeing has impurities in it. Now the drug's dangerous enough as it is because it can really unhinge people who are already emotionally unstable. But once you add something like strychnine, you can wind up with some pretty toxic stuff. So it's doubly dangerous." (:10)

Harris guessed that if LSD was in Lawrence, it was also showing up around the rest of the country. He said that it was possible there was a manufacturer in Kansas, but that it took a fairly skilled chemist to make the drug, moreso than for metamphetamines, a

73

manufacturer of which was recently discovered in Kansas City by police. Harris said that there were no local reports of the drug falling into the hands of children in grade school, although she had seen reports from elsewhere of acid-impregnated stamps showing cartoon characters.

You have the following videotape:

- Privette showing you evidence bags containing LSD capsules, shot at Kansas City DEA headquarters (up to :30).
- A group counseling session run in Lawrence by Harris, with six teen-agers who are recovering drug users, whose faces you can't show on camera (up to :20).
- The police testing lab in Kansas City, which determines the chemical makeup of confiscated drugs and material (up to :30).

Exercise written by John Broholm, broadcast journalism professor at the University of Kansas.

13-4. Simplify words

Broadcast writing depends on clarity and simplicity. One- or two syllable words are better than those with three or more syllables. Substitute these words for simpler ones.

1. utilize
2. interrogate
3. purchase
4. necessitate
5. deceased
6. terminate
7. contribute
8. perpetrator
9. apprehended
10. incarcerated

13-5. Rewrite sentences in active voice

Good writers try to use strong verbs and active voice in print journalism, but broadcast writing requires active voice even more. Change these sentences into active voice and strengthen the verbs when possible.

Passive: The fire was started by three boys, police said.
Active: Police say three boys started the fire.

1. The food chain owned by Carrs may be purchased by Safeway Inc.
2. Two apartment houses on the east side of town were destroyed by fire this morning.
3. Addiction to the Internet is considered a growing problem among college students by many professors.
4. There are several reasons offered by psychiatrists for the appeal of the Internet to college students.
5. There is an accident at the intersection of Northern Lights Boulevard and Bragaw Street almost every month.
6. At least 30 homes were destroyed in the fire that swept the hillside.
7. There are going to be several students who will have to drop out of school if tuition is increased.
8. An Anchorage man was shot by police after it was discovered that he killed a moose.
9. The lottery was won by two students.
10. The getaway car was driven by a perpetrator whom police suspect had been involved in several other robberies.

13-6. Brief news (Write a 15-second spot)

Write a brief 15-second spot (about five lines) based on this press release:

The Justice Club at (your university) will sponsor "Bringing Human Rights Home," on Tuesday, November 10 from 6 to 8:30 p.m. in Arts Building Room 150. Following a short documentary film featuring death row prisoner George McFarland and immigrant Jesus Collado, there will be a panel discussion with four panelists, and an open forum with the audience.

"Bringing Human Rights Home" will focus on the topics of the death penalty, immigrants' rights, prisoners' rights and habeas corpus relief. Speakers include Rich Curtner, Federal Defender for the state, and Robin Bronen, Director of Immigration and Refugee Services (Catholic Social Services Program).

13-7. News feature

Write a :30 (30 second) radio to TV news story based on the following press release. That's equivalent to about eight lines of typed copy or about 75 words.

Work out. Eat broccoli. Drink a glass of red wine. Smoke not at all. These fitness mantras are familiar. Now it seems that prayer, meditation, spiritual faith and communal worship may also be good for your health.

One study showed that patients with religious faith and social support are 12 times more likely to survive open-heart surgery. Another concluded that the mortality rate for people who attend religious services once a week is 25 to 35 percent lower than among those who worship less frequently. And clinical studies have confirmed a link between prayer and meditation, reduced blood pressure and heart rate.

Some people take this to mean there's a mind-body-spirit connection, says Tim Daaleman, an assistant professor of family medicine at the University of Kansas Medical Center. Critics think it demonstrates nothing but the healing power of suggestion and profound human gullibility.

Daaleman has a $240,000 Robert Wood Johnson Foundation grant to develop a test that will let researchers figure out how people's spiritual lives affect their sense of well-being. The work runs till the year 2001. So far, he has conducted 36 in-depth interviews, some with people who have a chronic illness, and drawn a few conclusions.

Those Daaleman studied didn't reach peace through sudden conversion. They got it from a deepening understanding of an existing belief system. Daaleman also found that a relationship to a higher power was more important than to a church or other religious group.

One of the most difficult kinds of prayer research concerns "intercessory prayer," the kind where you pray for somebody who's sick, for example. One study involved praying for alcoholics. "When word got out," Daaleman said, "there were people praying the study would fail. How do you control for that?"

Daaleman's wary of promoting the idea that spirituality's good for health. Somebody with appendicitis, for example, might rely on prayer when surgery's called for. But there are problems medicine can't touch, he said, like helping people with a terminal illness to find meaning. If spiritual tools help them cope, why not try to figure out what works best?

This stance won't make him popular. Some people will figure he should rest his faith in the Almighty and put his time to better use. Others will say that if he's earning a state salary he shouldn't study spiritual matters and scorch him on those grounds.

Web Writing 14

This chapter will give you practice in planning and writing stories for the Web. Use your creativity. Check sites you like for models. Two sites that offer inspiration are *www.fray.com* and *www.journale.com*. Check links to resources for online journalism on the book's Web site: http://info.wadsworth.com/rich.

14-1. Plan a Web project

Assume that you are planning a Web package for your campus newspaper or magazine. Using any of the topics suggested here or one you prefer, plan a storyboard for your package. Include links and interactive elements. You can also include multimedia elements. Be as creative as you wish. This is just a planning exercise; you don't have to produce this package. Some suggested topics:

- Increase in plagiarism on the Internet
- Binge drinking on college campuses
- Tuition increases at your university (with national comparisons)
- Campus crime (also consider national comparisons)
- Spring Break or any upcoming holiday
- Any topic of interest on your campus or in your community

14-2. Headlines and blurbs

Good headlines on the Web are crucial because readers have more competition for their attention on the Web than in print publications. Headlines should reveal the main idea of the story. If they are catchy to entice the reader, they must have a blurb that reveals the main idea. A brief headline of fewer than six to eight words is preferable to one that will span two lines.

Write headlines and blurbs for the following information; consider that your headline might stand alone on a Web page without the benefit of the blurb. Your blurb should be the lead you would create for the story or the nut graph.

a. A Harvard University professor disappeared more than a month ago. Yesterday (use the day of the week) his body was found in the Mississippi River at Vidalia, La. The body of Don Wiley, 57, was discovered snagged on a tree near a hydroelectric plant. His abandoned rental car had been found a few weeks earlier on a Mississippi River bridge at Memphis, Tenn., about 300 miles north of Vidalia. A wallet containing his identification was found on the body. Police said no evidence of foul play was found in the car.

b. A custodian at the Halliday, N.D., Public School District has become the head of the high school's science department. Ned Atkin started his first day at the rural school in western North Dakota wearing coveralls and boots, much like his uniform as the former custodian. "I didn't know if I was officially the janitor or a teacher that first morning I came in," he said. His promotion was due to an unexpected resignation of the district's only science teacher. Atkin has a degree in animal science.

c. The North Bend (Wash.) City Council passed an "inattentive drivers" ordinance yesterday to target people who violate traffic laws because they were distracted by eating, smoking, reading or talking on cell phones. It will also apply to people who put on makeup or otherwise don't watch the roads. The law takes effect Jan. 1 in this town about 30 miles east of Seattle. Police can already cite motorists for negligent driving, but this new ordinance spells out specific activities that could lead to fines.

d. They're blaming it on loose laws and a cowboy culture. Whatever the cause, the facts are that people on Montana's roads are more likely to die in alcohol-related crashes than motorists in any other state except Mississippi. Montana ranks second in the nation as the highest rate of alcohol-related traffic deaths. Montana has resisted lowering the legal blood-alcohol rate from 0.10 percent to .08 percent as more than half of the other states in the country have done. And Montana allows open alcoholic-beverage containers in vehicles outside cities. That means drivers can have a beer or other alcoholic drink while they drive on the highways.

e. A new Web site has been created for kittens and cats. The site is geared to cats that are fascinated with moving objects. The site gives cats a choice of three objects to chase: a bird, a bee and a butterfly, each with sounds such as a chirping sound for the bird, a buzzing sound for the bee and a whirring sound for the butterfly. Steve Malarkey, the site designer, said many cats like to chase the cursor on computer screens, so this is just an alternative. The site is *www.cattv.com.*

14-3. Web briefs

Online readers want their information in many forms – headline only, summary blurb, briefs, full story or extended information. For a news story, you might just summarize the first few paragraphs. Write these stories as complete briefs, preferably with a catchy ending. Write the briefs as directed – some are only a sentence or two while others are a few paragraphs.

a. Write a brief of one or two sentences based on the following information:

A Colorado State University professor of environmental health has studied the lifestyles of 51 dogs with lung cancer. John Reif, the researcher, found that dogs with short noses are 50 percent more likely to develop lung cancer when they live with owners who smoke. The researchers also studied 83 dogs with other forms of cancer. Reif is using the dogs as models to study the environmental effects of smoke on human beings. He said the study confirms findings that exposure to environmental tobacco smoke increases the risk of human lung cancer. Reif found that long-nosed dogs, such as collies and retrievers, seemed to be protected against passive smoke. The study appeared in the American Journal of Epidemiology. Reif is also studying the effects of pesticides on dogs.

b. Write a two-paragraph brief based on the following information.

A University of South Florida professor is operating the country's first solar-powered vehicle. Professor Lee Stefanakos is chairman of USF's electrical engineering department. He is operating the vehicle at the university's Tampa campus, which is the test site for a fleet of 12 electric vans, cars and trucks. The vehicles get their energy from the sun. The vehicles have solar panels mounted in a carport roof. The solar-powered cars come equipped with air conditioning and other options. The vehicles cover up to 60 miles on a charge and can reach speeds up to 55 miles per hour. The cost of operating the vehicles is about 4 cents per mile. The cost of operating a gasoline-powered car is about 40 cents a mile. The solar-powered cars have 36 batteries mounted under the vehicle. They weigh a total of 1,200 pounds. "Florida does not have any energy resource of its own except the sun, so it makes sense to use it," Stefanakos said. The university received a $1 million grant from the U.S. Department of Energy to study ways to make motorists less dependent on gasoline.

Based on a story from the Sun-Sentinel, (Fort Lauderdale, Fla.) Used with permission.

14-4. Chunk-style writing with cliffhangers

Some online readers prefer chunk-style stories that span several pages with each page contained on one or two screens and links at the bottom that entice the readers to continue. Those links or the last sentence of the chunk should be written as a cliffhanger – a sentence or paragraph that provides some mystery. Write this story in chunk style with cliffhangers at the end of each chunk. Limit your story to about three chunks with each chunk no more than one or two screens. Here is the information, which is not well worded or in good order:

The event took place at National Furniture Liquidators at 1202 Maple Grove Road.

A skunk wandered through the open door of the store on Monday afternoon. Throughout the day, store employees tried to catch it. By 8 p.m. the store closed and the skunk was still at large. Efforts to capture it had failed.

The store has thousands of dollars worth of overstuffed chairs, sofas and loveseats. When the skunk first walked in, Dennis Goke, acting assistant manager, wasn't taking any chances. So for the first hour, the skunk was allowed run of the place. It wandered up and down warehouse aisles while employees eyeballed it warily from the doorway. As customers pulled into the parking lot, they were greeted by the unsettling warning of "Hey, we got a loose skunk in here!"

Originally when the skunk walked in three employees did what anyone would do. They hid. Through the rest of the day, although the employees stayed outside more than in, the store didn't close. Business continued throughout the afternoon, if not exactly business as usual.

"If it would have been a squirrel, I would have chased him out with a broom," Goke said.

At one point, the employees tried to lure it out with a trail of whole wheat bread crumbs, but the skunk wasn't hungry. However, the crumbs attracted dozens of gulls, which screeched and screamed and flapped and gorged until most of the bread was gone.

"I've worked in strange situations before," Goke said. "I've worked in floods. I've worked without any power in the building." But none of those circumstances had the opportunity to wreak as much havoc as a skunk.

Store manager Bill Frolichman, who had been on vacation, arrived late in the afternoon to oversee the situation. He decided to wait until closing, then tried to spook out the skunk with bright lights and rock music.

Earlier in the day, after the attempts by employees to lure the skunk out failed, Rich Ulkus of Animal Allies arrived to see what he could do. By then the skunk had had enough. There were too many people around and too much commotion. It disappeared into hiding somewhere in the bowels of the store.

That made employees more nervous than watching it roam the aisles.

Ulkus spent a few minutes on his hands and knees, shining a floodlight under some of the couches and drawing gasps of admiration and comments about his bravery from the others, but he couldn't find the skunk, so he and Goke baited a trap with tuna, wrapped the tuna in several layers of plastic, then wrapped the whole thing in a blanket and stuck it in a corner.

Based on a story from The (Duluth, Minn.) *News-Tribune.* Used with permission.

80

14-5. Web news story

Web usabilities experts mentioned in your textbook recommend writing online stories with boldfaced subheads, lists and inverted pyramid style to help readers scan material. Although those recommendations don't need to apply to all stories, they are helpful for many basic news stories. Put a space between paragraphs. Use those techniques to write this story based on a press release from the U.S. Department of Commerce. Add a headline and summary blurb. Write short paragraphs and condense this story to one page – about two or three computer screens, depending on the margins.

The U.S. Department of Justice's National Institute of Justice and the Bureau of Justice Statistics released a report today. The report, "The Sexual Victimization of College Women," offers a comprehensive look into the prevalence and nature of sexual assault occurring at American colleges. The federally funded study was conducted by Bonnie S. Fisher, a professor at the University of Cincinnati. The report may be obtained from the National Institute of Justice Web site at *http://www.ojp.usdoj.gov/nij/*. Additional criminal justice materials can be obtained from the Office of Justice home page at *http://www.ojp.usdoj.gov.*

The study showed that about 3 percent of college women experience a completed and/or attempted rape during a college year. The data show that about 1.7 percent of female college students were victims of attempted rape. About 1.7 percent of the college women reported being coerced to have sex. The study also estimated that about 13 percent of college women have been stalked since the beginning of the school year. Of the incidents of sexual victimization, the vast majority occurred after 6 p.m. in living quarters. For completed rapes, nearly 60 percent that took place on campus occurred in the victim's residence, 31 percent occurred in other living quarters on campus and 10 percent occurred at a fraternity. Most off-campus victimization, especially rapes, also occurred in residences. However, particularly for sexual contacts and threatened victimizations, incidents also took place in bars, dance clubs, nightclubs and work settings. Most of the sexually assaulted women knew the person who victimized them.

The National Institute of Justice and the Bureau of Justice Statistics are components of the Office of Justice Programs, which also includes the Bureau of Justice Assistance, the Office of Juvenile Justice and Delinquency Prevention, and the Office for Victims of Crime.

Based on their findings, Bonnie Fisher and her colleagues estimate that the women at a college that has 10,000 female students could experience more than 350 rapes a year-- a finding with serious policy implications for college administrators. Fisher also found that many women do not characterize their sexual victimizations as a crime for a number of reasons (such as embarrassment, not clearly understanding the legal definition of rape, or not wanting to define someone they know who victimized them as a rapist) or because they blame themselves for their sexual assault. The study reinforces the importance of many organizations' efforts to improve education and knowledge about sexual assault.

Attention to the sexual victimization of college women, however, also has been prompted by the rising fear that college campuses are not ivory towers but, instead, have become hot spots for criminal activity. Researchers have shown that college campuses and their students are not free from the risk of criminal victimization. Previous research suggests that these women are at greater risk for rape and other forms of sexual assault than women in the general population or in a comparable age group. College women might, therefore, be a group whose victimization warrants special attention.

Who was surveyed?

NCWSV study results are based on a telephone survey of a randomly selected, national sample of 4,446 women who were attending a 2- or 4-year college or university. The sample was limited to schools with at least 1,000 students. Furthermore, from a policy perspective, college administrators might be disturbed to learn that for every 1,000 women attending their institutions, there may well be 35 incidents of rape in a given academic year (based on a victimization rate of 35.3 per 1,000 college women). For a campus with 10,000 women, this would mean the number of rapes could exceed 350. Even more broadly, when projected over the Nation's female student population of several million, these figures suggest that rape victimization is a potential problem of large proportion and of public policy interest.

Accuracy and Libel   15

This chapter will test your knowledge of some basic principles of libel. No exercise can substitute for the fact checking you should do before you turn in your stories. You should always check the spelling of names and make sure that you have spelled a source's name correctly in all references. You should also check facts, such as dates, and make sure your quotes are used in the proper context. Check the Web site for this book for online resources and an interactive, self-graded libel quiz: *http://info.wadsworth.com/rich.*

15-1. Libel quiz

Circle the correct answers.

1. The textbook has listed four defenses against libel (truth, Sullivan, privilege, fair comment and criticism). From a reporter's point of view, which is the strongest and why?

    a. Truth

    b. Sullivan

    c. Privilege

    d. Fair comment and criticism

2. With respect to libel law, what does "actual malice" mean?

    a. That the reporter was careless

    b. That the reporter tried to be mean to the plaintiff

    c. That the reporter was negligent

    d. That the reporter made a false statement either knowing the information was wrong or with reckless disregard for whether it was wrong

3. The "actual malice" standard comes into play in a libel suit

    a. with private figure plaintiffs who cannot prove negligence.

    b. with plaintiffs who are public officials or public figures.

    c. only when the newspaper refuses to print a correction.

    d. only when the newspaper sues a public official for libel.

4. Which of the following is *not* a reason the Supreme Court established the "actual malice" test in Sullivan?

    a. To encourage robust debate on public issues

    b. To encourage a free press to publish matters of public concern

    c. In recognition that important public debate may include vehement, caustic and sharp attacks on public officials

    d. In recognition that in a democracy, private figures, too, have to be ready for sharp or unpleasant attacks in the press

5. With respect to libel law, "privilege" means

    a. you can report anything in a public place without worrying about checking facts.

    b. you can go on private property to gather information.

    c. you may print defamatory statements from a public proceeding or public record as long as you are being fair and accurate.

    d. you have the absolute privilege to report the news, guaranteed by the First Amendment.

6. As a news photographer, you use a telephoto lens to shoot pictures in your neighbor's back yard, some 300 feet from your location on a public sidewalk.

    a. You may be guilty of invasion of privacy under the intrusion category.

    b. You are protected from any action because you're a journalist.

    c. Your neighbor can sue you for libel if you print a topless picture of her.

    d. You are protected from an invasion of privacy – public disclosure of private facts action because you've taken the information from a public place, and that is the same as the public record.

7. Your advertising department wants to use a picture of the hometown baseball hero in an automobile dealer advertisement.

    a. Since he's a public figure, the ad people can simply clip a photo from the files and put it in without notifying the hometown hero.

    b. The ad people can use him because he is newsworthy.

    c. The ad people have to receive his permission and pay him if he requests it, since this is for commercial purposes.

    d. This could be considered an invasion of privacy under false light publicity.

8. You have been sued for invasion of privacy – public disclosure of private facts – for publishing a person's less than flattering mental health history. You will likely win the suit if

    a. you took the information from a public record.

    b. the person's physician said it was OK to use the information.

    c. you print a retraction.

    d. you obtained the document from an anonymous source.

9. With respect to accuracy, experienced journalists

    a. don't worry about it too much since the Sullivan defense is there to protect them.

    b. usually check the major facts, then "go with their gut."

    c. check details, even little things, to see if a source or story "doesn't add up."

    d. know the "corrections" column is there to back them up.

10. Showing your copy to sources before it is published

    a. is never permitted.

    b. is a sign that you doubt the truth of your story.

    c, will lead to a lawsuit.

    d. is a way that some journalists catch inaccuracies before publication.

This exercise was written by Tom Volek, media law professor at the University of Kansas.

15-2. Libel quiz #2

Using your computer, write brief answers to the following questions:

1. What is the difference between libel and slander?

2. What are the three types of public figures? Define each type.

3. In *Hutchinson v. Proxmire,* on what grounds did the court rule that Hutchinson was not a public figure?

4. If a public official sues a newspaper for libel, what does the official have to prove to the court?

5. How do the standards for proving libel differ for a public official and a private individual in many states?

6. Define absolute privilege.

7. Define qualified privilege.

8. What are the four grounds for invasion of privacy suits?

9. In *Dietemann v. Time Inc.,* why did the court rule in favor of Dietemann?

10. What is the purpose of the Uniform Corrections Act and what type of correction would a publication have to run if it is sued for libel?

15-3. Online legal issues

Answer the following questions by writing true or false.

1. _____ If someone posts a libelous message to an online discussion group without using his or her real name, the Internet service provider is responsible for the liability.

2. _____ The U.S. Supreme Court ruled that the Communications Decency Act of 1996 could restrict distribution of indecent material on the Internet to people under age 18.

3. _____ The U.S. Supreme Court ruled that the entire Communications Decency Act of 1996 was unconstitutional.

4. _____ In *Zeran v. AOL,* the U.S. Supreme Court ruled that America Online was not responsible for the death threats and defamatory messages that Kenneth Zeran received concerning the Oklahoma City bombing of a federal building.

5. _____ If you take a picture from the Internet from a site that does not have a copyright symbol on it, the information is copyright-free.

6. _____ If you post a home page on the Internet without using a copyright symbol, you are protected by the U.S. copyright laws.

7. _____ The No Electronic Theft Act allows you to copy software and online materials as long as you don't make a profit.

8. _____ If a site is encrypted, that means it contains special codes that only government agents can read.

9. _____ When you buy things online, you should check whether the site is encrypted before you send your credit card information.

10. _____ You can post any type of message on a discussion even if it is libelous because online discussion groups do not qualify as "publication" under the standards applied to libel cases.

Ethics

16

Journalists have to make difficult decisions in the course of doing their duty. It is not always possible to serve the public without causing harm to someone. However, you can minimize harm if you use some moral reasoning guidelines to justify your actions. Using some of the principles in the textbook, consider the following cases.

These cases are based on real dilemmas reporters, photographers and editors faced at *The Hartford Courant,* where Henry McNulty was the reader representative. It was his job to respond to readers' concerns and complaints. As the former ombudsman for the newspaper, he often had to justify why the newspaper made some difficult decisions. McNulty periodically wrote a column in which he asked readers to play the role of editor and make a decision about dilemmas the journalists faced. Here are some cases McNulty presented to his readers. You be the editor; choose one of these options or devise an alternative to them and justify your decision.

The Internet is creating many new ethical dilemmas for journalists. You can access many ethics resources and codes of ethics with links on the book's Web site at: *http://info.wadsworth.com/rich.*

16-1. The bad joke

Your reporter is covering a speech by a local politician. The politician makes a joke in the speech that offends several members of the audience, who stand up and walk out. The person covering the speech reports this, but in the story repeats the joke told by the politician. It has a sexual theme. In editing the story:

- ❑ You delete the joke because you consider it offensive and inappropriate for your newspaper.
- ❑ You let it stand on the grounds that otherwise your readers (or viewers) can't properly judge the actions of the politician and those people who walked out.

16-2. The telephone number

Your newspaper is about to publish a wire-service story about the "Overground Railroad," a network that would help women get abortions if *Roe v. Wade* were to be overturned. The story is neutral as to whether the right to an abortion should exist, but it includes, at the end, the toll-free number for the Overground Railroad headquarters. In editing the story:

- ❑ You let the phone number stand. You reason that it's simply a way to help interested readers, similar to printing the opening hours of an art exhibit. It's not free advertising, you argue, nor does it promote abortion.
- ❑ You delete the phone number. If the subject were non-controversial, you wouldn't object to providing this information. But the story deals with abortion, one of the most hotly debated issues of the day. And besides, other stories haven't had the phone number for groups like Operation Rescue.

16-3. Son of superintendent

A 20-year-old man in your city is arrested on morals charges involving a 17-year-old girl. Your reporter writes the story, and it includes the fact that the arrested person is the son of the superintendent of schools. In editing it:

- ❑ You leave in the mention of the father, because you believe this fact is important to readers. The father is well-known locally, and such unpleasant publicity is one of the prices of fame. Also, you don't want to be accused of covering up anything touching on a public official.
- ❑ You delete the reference to the father. He is in no way connected to the arrest, and you reason that to report the family connection would be unfair.

Cases from *The Hartford* (Conn.) *Courant.* Reprinted with permission.

16-4. A hero's private life

Imagine that you are the editor of your newspaper. Write your justification for the following ethical dilemma as though you had to explain it to your readers (or viewers) in a column on the editorial page or next to the story.

A woman armed with a gun takes aim at the president, but a man intervenes by deflecting her arm. Later, after the newspapers report the news incident, a newspaper writes about the man and identifies him as gay. He had not revealed his sexual preference to his family, and he is upset by this revelation. However, he has become a national hero. As the editor of the newspaper, would you have printed this information about his personal life? Justify your decision.

16-5. Anonymous sources

Your textbook describes an ethical dilemma the editors at the *Seattle Times* faced when eight women accused former U.S. Sen. Brock Adams of sexual harassment. The women refused to allow their names to be used. The senator was running for re-election. Would you have printed the story using anonymous sources? Justify your decision. Write your views in a column, just as Michael Fancher, editor of the Seattle newspaper, did when he published this story. When the scandal between President Clinton and Monica Lewinsky first broke, the media relied heavily on anonymous sources. Would you have used anonymous sources to report these initial findings?

16-6. Cooperating with police

You are the police reporter for your local newspaper. Police have informed you that they plan to make a sweep of arrests for prostitution at a local park. They ask you to publish the names of the persons they arrest, including the men who solicit the prostitutes. They say that prostitution is a major problem in your community and by publishing the names of the "johns," you can help deter this crime. Your newspaper normally does not publish the names of persons arrested on minor morals charges. What are the ethical problems this case presents? Will you publish the names? Justify your decision by writing pros and cons and discussing harms versus benefits.

16-7. Personal dilemma

Study the ethical guidelines in your textbook. Discuss a personal dilemma you have had either on an internship or during the course of your education. Would you make the same decision now, after using ethical guidelines, as you did at the time?

16-8. Code of ethics

Working in groups, create a code of ethics for your campus newspaper. Check the codes of ethics of journalism organizations by linking to them from the Web site for this book. Devise your own code using some of these topics:
- Use of deception
- Accepting gifts or free tickets
- Anonymous sources
- Altering photographs
- Conflicts of interest – socializing with sources.

16-9. Online ethical issues

Discuss new ethical dilemmas that are being creating by online media, such as the following:

- Would you or should you quote sources from newsgroups without their permission?
- Should you include links to online plagiarism sites in news stories about the problems of plagiarism on the Internet because of easy access to so much information?
- Should you link to pornographic sites in a news story about the proliferation and popularity of such sites on the Internet? Does it make a difference if your publication is on a university server or is a campus online newspaper or magazine?
- Should you include e-mail messages posted to discussion lists in news stories?
- Would you fire an employee who plagiarized information? If not, how would you handle a case of a reporter who lifted information from another source from online sources without permission?

Multicultural Sensitivity 17

This chapter is designed to increase your sensitivity to the concerns of people from many ethnic, racial and minority groups and to become aware of gender issues in the media. However, the best way to understand people who differ from you is to talk to them and ask them about their concerns as they relate to the media and to the way they are treated in society. Many ethnic and racial media organizations have Web sites offering networking and sources. You can link to them from the Web site for this book: *<http://info.wadsworth.com/rich>*.

17-1. Media survey

If your instructor prefers, you may do this as a class project with each student assigned to a different organization.

Part 1: Conduct a survey of the media in your community and/or state (newspapers, magazines, television stations, advertising and public relations firms) to determine the number of minorities and women in various positions. How many minorities do these organizations employ in news/editorial positions? How many of these minorities or women are in management positions (as editors, for example)? How many minorities or women are in top management positions – managing editors, executive editors, news directors, publishers, and so on? How does this percentage or figure compare with the total number of minorities in the organization, and what types of jobs do the majority of minorities have?

Part 2: Interview top editors of these organizations and ask them if they have any official policies regarding recruiting and hiring of minorities and women in general staff positions and in management positions. Ask editors (or top officials) to explain any efforts they have taken to increase minority representation at their organizations. If they say they are looking for qualified minorities and women, ask them to explain their definition of "qualified."

17-2. Photo sensitivity

Analyze the photographs of minorities – particularly African-Americans, Hispanic-Americans, Asian-Americans or Native Americans – in your local newspaper or other newspapers for a week or more.   Do they perpetuate stereotypes?   (Make copies of some of the photographs you selected.) To understand the issue, read the following material before you do your analysis.

Many studies and articles criticize the media for using photographs that portray minorities in a negative light, such as photos portraying African-Americans in crime scenes.

17-3. Gender stereotypes

Analyze how men and women are portrayed in commercials on television. Be on the lookout for male bashing as much as for female stereotyping. Write the name of the advertiser, a brief description and whether or not you believe the advertisement portrays men and women in stereotypical or sexist ways. If possible, watch the ads with a person of the opposite sex to compare your perceptions. Here are some qualities to look for:

- Are women portrayed in commercials set in the kitchen more than men? Are men being portrayed as inferior to make women look strong, intelligent or superior?
- Are women being used as sex symbols in commercials for products unrelated to physical appearance?
- In commercials about physical appearance such as dieting, are more women featured than men?
- What stereotypes do you think these commercials perpetuate?
- How many of the commercials feature men and women of different races and what types of commercials are they?

17-4. Age perceptions

Throughout this textbook you have been cautioned to avoid adjectives and, instead, favor concrete images of people in action or anecdotes that illustrate a point. This is particularly true when you are trying to be sensitive to multicultural issues. However, for this exercise you will be asked to consider the use of some adjectives just to test your perceptions about age. Make sure you list your own age. Or you can give this exercise to someone much older or much younger than you and see if the results differ. Place the number for an age group next to the following nouns or adjectives. You may use one age group more than once. Compare your choices with those of your classmates and discuss whether age perceptions vary and why.

Noun/Adjective	Age
_____ Baby	(1) Less than 1
_____ Infant	(2) 1 to 2
_____ Toddler	(3) 2+ to 3
_____ Child	(4) 3+ to 4
_____ Youth	(5) 4+ to 5
_____ Kid	(6) 5+ to 6
_____ Teenager	(7) 6+ to 10
_____ Young	(8) 10+ to 12
_____ Middle Age	(9) 13 to 19
_____ Old	(10) 20 to 24
_____ Baby boomers	(11) 25 to 29
_____ Elderly	(12) 30 to 39
_____ Senior citizen	(13) 40 to 49
_____ Woman	(14) 50 to 59
_____ Man	(15) 60 to 69
_____ Girl	(16) 70 to 79
_____ Boy	(17) 80 to 89
_____ Octogenarian	(18) 90 to 100
	(19) Over 100

Your age_____   Your sex: Male(_____)   Female(_____)

Beat Reporting 18

This chapter will give you practice generating beat story ideas and concepts for beat coverage in print and on-line publications. Check the Web site for this book for many sources for beat reporters: *http://info.wadsworth.com/rich.*

Using the tips in your textbook for starting a beat, write sources and story ideas as follows:

18-1. Finding story ideas for your beat

1. Choose a beat that you would like to cover on campus, preferably one not covered by the campus newspaper.

_____

2. List at least three major sources you would contact regularly to cover this beat.

a. _____

b. _____

c. _____

3. List three people related to your beat who would make good profiles.

a. _____

b. _____

c. _____

4. Find three story ideas from bulletin boards or press releases from this beat.

a. _____

b. _____

c. _____

5. Interview at least five to 10 students or residents of your community about story ideas for your beat. Ask these sources what kinds of stories they want to read that pertain to your beat, what kinds of stories they don't see covered in the newspapers now, and what types of stories they would prefer. Ask also for suggestions of at least one story idea from every person you interview.

18-2. Briefs or press releases

Based on the information you found from bulletin boards or press releases in the previous assignment, write two news briefs. If you are a public relations major and your instructor permits, write the information as press releases instead of news briefs.

18-3. Analyze beat coverage

Read your local or campus newspaper for a week and write the types of stories covered on a beat of your choice. Are most of the stories based on breaking news from press releases, press conferences or upcoming events? Are most of the stories feature articles? What types of stories are missing and what changes would you recommend?

18-4. Analyze a beat story

Analyze a beat story in your campus or local newspaper by making a list of reporting questions the writer might have asked to get the information in the story. Now add questions you think the reporter should have asked to get additional information you would want to know. What online information should supplement the story?

18-5. Team beats

1. Several newspapers throughout the country have revamped their beat coverage by creating new beats that are based on readers' interests and by organizing reporters in teams. Using your campus or local newspaper as a base of readers, devise four new team beats that you think would serve your campus or community. For example, the student life beat, which could encompass entertainment, housing, recreation and other facets of student life.

a. _____

b. _____

c. _____

d. _____

2. Dividing the class into groups, choose one team beat per group (or whatever numbers work for the class). Devise three story ideas for your group's team beat.

a. _____

b. _____

c. _____

18-6. Online newspaper beats

1. Online newspapers are geared to reader interactivity. Using any beat you prefer, either a team or personal beat, devise three ideas for reader interaction. For example, you might consider a trivia quiz or a question related to a story.

a. _____

b. _____

c. _____

2. Write at least five ideas for information related to your beat that could be kept in an archive of an online newspaper, such as key statistics about athletes, names and information about campus or other public officials, where to get permits or other needed documents, and other consumer information about your school or community.

a. _____

b. _____

c. _____

d. _____

e. _____

18-7. Analysis of beat resources

Web resources created for journalists by journalists abound, and these directories can save you time and energy hunting for online beat resources. This exercise is designed to familiarize you with some of these outstanding directories, which are linked to the book Web site for this chapter: *http://info.wadsworth.com/rich.*

Write a brief summary and analysis of the following journalism directories; include a paragraph or two describing the directory and its contents and a few paragraphs rating the value of the directory.

1. A Journalist's Guide to the Internet: *http://reporter.umd.edu/*

2. Power Reporting: *http://powerreporting.com*

3. Reporter's Desktop: *http://www.reporter.org/desktop/*

4. IRE's Beat Resource Guide:

   http://www.ire.org/resourcecenter/initial-search-beat.html/

5. Facsnet: *http://www.facsnet.org/*

6. Society of Environmental Journalists: *http://www.sej.org/*

7. Education Writers' Association: *http://www.ewa.org/*

8. JournalismNet: *http://www.journalismnet.com/*

9. Radio and Television News Directors' Association (newsroom

   resources): *http://www.rtnda.org/*

10. Society of Professional Journalists (resources): *http://www.spj.org/*

Obituaries

19

These exercises will give you practice writing standard-form obituaries and feature obituaries. Use the examples in your textbook as models. Include the cause of death and courtesy titles, even though many newspapers may not require either. Use Associated Press style, not the style in the death notices, which are often written and paid for by the family or funeral home and do not follow newspaper style. Omit the flowery language and euphemisms. People die. They don't "enter into rest," "depart," or "pass away." Write the obituaries as directed. Check the Web site for this book for online resources: *http://info.wadsworth.com/rich.*

19-1. Basic obituaries

a. Your editor asks you to check the death notices (announcements usually submitted by funeral homes of funerals or other services) and write obituaries from them. Write this obituary in standard form with courtesy titles for the person who died, male or female. This information is adapted from an obituary published in *The Oregonian,* but the name of the deceased and addresses have been changed.

Samuel Morris Burnside, beloved father of Harold G. of Salem and Dr. Robert M. of Springfield; devoted grandfather of 10 grandchildren, eight great-grandchildren; and two great-great-grandchildren, passed away Monday. He was a retired real estate broker and past president and lieutenant governor of Division 64 of Kiwanis Pacific Northwest District. Funeral services, 1 p.m. Friday in the chapel of Young's Funeral Home, 640 Broad St., in Tigard. Burial in Crescent Grove Cemetery, 320 Main St., Portland. The family suggests remembrances be contributions to Southwest Hills Kiwanis Club.

You call the funeral home and the family and get this additional information:
He was born April 29, 1920. The family says the cause of death is heart failure. He died in the Portland Care Center in Southwest Portland where he had resided for the last 10 years. He was born in Weber, Utah, and grew up on a farm near Grant, Idaho. He moved to Portland from Jerome, Idaho, in 1942.

He attended the University of Idaho and Albin State Normal School. He retired many years ago but had worked as a real estate broker in the Southwest Portland area for many years.

He was past president and lieutenant governor of Division 64 of Kiwanis Pacific Northwest District. Survivors include his sons, Harold G. of Salem and Dr. Robert M. of Springfield; 10 grandchildren, eight great-grandchildren; and two great-great-grandchildren.

Based on an obituary from *The Oregonian.* Used with permission.

b. Your editor wants you to advance this obituary by starting with the funeral arrangements because the person died five days earlier. Use courtesy titles for the deceased and cause of death. Be sure to follow Associated Press style, not the style in the following death notice from the funeral home. Note AP style for states, not Postal Service style. Use the simpler word "burial" instead of "interment."

Sandra K. Sullivan, beloved daughter of Zoe Margolis, loving mother of sons, Christopher and Vernon of [your town] and Archie of Lansing, MI.; and daughter Mattie Hills of San Francisco, CA., died Saturday. Leaves numerous nieces and nephews. She was born June 12, 1950. A native of (your town) and lifelong resident, she devoted herself to helping others. Friends are welcome for Visitation Friday from 9 A.M. to 9 P.M. and are respectfully invited to attend Funeral Services Saturday at 10 A.M. in the St. Paul's Baptist Church, 9030 Addison Place, [Your town]. Private interment. Remembrances may be made to the Sandra K. Sullivan musical scholarships at the church.

You call the family and funeral home. You notice that Sandra Sullivan is survived by her mother and children, but there is no mention of a husband in the death notice. You ask how she would prefer to be addressed, and her family tells you to use "Ms." Other information from the family and funeral home includes:

Cause of death – cancer. She died in her home.

Occupation: She was director of the private Foundation for Independent Living in your town, an organization that helps disabled people. She worked for the organization for 20 years and was director for the past 10 years. She was also an accomplished pianist and choir musical director for St. Paul's Baptist Church. She graduated from the high school in your town and earned a bachelor's degree in social work from Michigan State University and a master's degree in social work from New York University.

She was divorced in 1980 from Harry G. Sullivan, but her family says they do not want that mentioned in the obituary.

c. This information is also from a paid death notice. You supplement it with interviews from the family. Use courtesy titles and cause of death. Make sure you check AP style for abbreviations of states, and avoid euphemisms for death. In AIDS cases, sometimes you face an ethical decision whether to state the cause of death. In this case, the deceased was an advocate for the disease.

Brett Stephen Huff entered into rest Monday. Beloved son of Martha and Edward Huff [of your town], and beloved brother of John of Ames, IA.; James of Scarsdale, N.Y., and Joseph of Dallas, TX.; dearly beloved grandson of Mary Margaret Huff, and nephew of Linda May Love of Detroit, MI. He was born [in your town] in 1970 and graduated from [your town's high school]. He earned a bachelor's degree in art from the University of Missouri in Columbia, MO. He owned his own graphics design firm [in your city] and had designed many brochures for area firms. A Mass of Christian Burial will be celebrated at 10:30 A.M. [use the day of the week for tomorrow] at Our Savior Church, 2020 Marysville Ave. Burial will be in Greenlawn Cemetery, 30 Main Street, [your town].   Contributions may be made to the AIDS Research Fund, Fernwood Hospital, 373 Paloma Street, [your town].

You suspect the cause of death is related to AIDS, and you call the family for information. Huff's mother confirms that he had AIDS. She says he died at her home [in your town]. She tells you that in the past year that he had spoken to school students in many area high schools to educate them about the disease. He was diagnosed with AIDS in 1994 when he was living in Los Angeles. He had worked for the Tucker Design Group in that city, but in 1995 he moved your city to be near his family, and he started his own firm, Huff Designs. "He wanted to alert people to ways of preventing AIDS," his mother says. "He tried to make people more sensitive to people who have the disease."

19-2. Feature obituary - Jerry Garcia

Write a feature obituary based on this information and any additional information you may gather. The day Jerry Garcia died, thousands of his fans flooded the Internet with messages of mourning and memories. You can gain additional information by using the World Wide Web on the Internet. You can find a home page for the Grateful Dead as well as several sites on the Web devoted to Garcia. The easiest way to locate these sites is to use a search engine, such as *www.google.com;* just type in Jerry Garcia, and sites will come up.

Here is some basic information from a variety of obituaries and articles about Garcia. Consider the ethical issue of whether you would include information about his drug use. When you include quotes by him or about him from previous interviews, attribute your source. Although the exact date of death is given here, use yesterday as your time frame.

Basic factual information:

Who: Jerome John Garcia, better known as "Jerry," the lead guitarist of the rock band, the Grateful Dead, died Aug. 9, 1995.

Age: 53

When: 4:23 a.m. (Pacific time – 7:23 a.m. EDT)

Where: In his bed at Serenity Knolls, a residential treatment center for drug addiction in Forest Knolls, Marin County, Calif.

Cause of death: Heart attack, according to the Marin County sheriff's office

Garcia had suffered from diabetes and general ill health for several years. He was an admitted user of heroin and psychedelic drugs such as LSD.

Survivors: Wife, Deborah Koons Garcia, a Marin County filmmaker, four daughters: Heather, 32, Annabelle, 25, Teresa, 21 and Keelin, 6.

Funeral arrangements: Undecided at this time.

Background:

Born Jerome John Garcia in San Francisco on Aug. 1, 1942. Son of a band leader, Jose. Garcia was 5 when he witnessed the drowning death of his father. About that time Garcia lost the tip of his right middle finger in a wood-chopping accident. He was raised primarily by his mother, Ruth, who ran a saloon near the San Francisco waterfront. Became interested in playing electric guitar and painting when he was 15. Was a devoted reader of Beat Generation writer, Jack Kerouac. Quit high school after one year, worked as a salesman and a teacher for a while and joined the Army. After an early discharge, took classes at what is now the San Francisco Art Institute. Years later his abstract art was marketed in a line of neckties that earned him more than $30 million. Garcia even had an ice cream named after him, Ben & Jerry's Cherry Garcia ice cream.

Garcia formed the Warlocks rock group in 1964. This group became the Grateful Dead in 1966. Original members were Garcia, guitarist Bob Weir, Ron "Pigpen" McKernan, who died of a liver ailment in 1973, bass player Phil Lesh and drummer Bill Kreutzman. Drummer Mickey Hart joined n 1967. It was a group that combined rock, bluegrass, blues and folk influences. Garcia was lead guitarist, composer and sometime vocalist. Among the band's best known songs were "Truckin'," "Casey Jones," and "Friend of the Devil." Its only top 10 hit was the 1987 song "Touch of Grey." The name "Warlocks" was already taken. In an interview with *Rolling Stone,* Garcia said, "We never decided to be the Grateful Dead. What happened was the Grateful Dead came up as a suggestion because we were at Phil's house one day; he had a big Oxford dictionary, I opened it up and the first thing I saw was The Grateful Dead. It said that on the page and it was so astonishing. It was truly weird, a truly weird moment." A grateful dead is a type of traditional British folk ballad in which a human helps a ghost of someone who has died recently find peace.

From *People* magazine: Garcia once reportedly said about psychedelic drugs: "I don't think there's anything else in life apart from a near-death experience that shows you how extensive the mind is."

In a 1993 interview with *The New Yorker,* he said he had given up drugs and taken up scuba diving. "It's an ecstatic experience," he said of scuba diving. "I love it almost as much as I love music."

From an interview with KFOG-FM in 1993: "Ideally I would just like to disappear gracefully and not leave behind any legacy to hang people up. I don't want people agonizing over who or what I was when I was here when I'm not here anymore. I would like to be thought of as a competent musician. That would be good. I'd like that."

In the past few years he had stopped smoking, cut down on drugs, and hired a personal fitness trainer.

The Grateful Dead was much more than a band. To millions of devoted fans, known as "Deadheads," it was a way of life. Many of these fans followed the group from concert to concert. The band was one of the most popular ever on the concert tour, grossing tens of millions of dollars each year from its concerts.

Based on information from The Associated Press and other sources.

19-3. Online obituary

Newspapers and major broadcast outlets often prepare advanced obituaries on famous people. Online obituaries can include the basic feature information and links to timelines and related sites.

Using a celebrity, politician or entertainer who is still alive, search the Internet for information and write a feature obituary. Include links to other sites. An easy way to do this is to open your word processor and when you link to a related site you would like to use, copy the URL (highlight the URL, pull down your Edit menu to copy), then open your document in your word processor and paste the URL.

19-4. Style quiz

Correct the errors in the following sentences:

1. He is survived by his sons in Lansing, MI. and a daughter in Dallas, TX.

2. Jim Henson began appearing on television with the Muppets in the 1960's.

3. Funeral services will be held at 1 P.M. Friday.

4. A mass of Christian burial will be held at 10:30 a.m. Thursday.

5. She passed away on September 9, 1992.

6. Father James Flanagan is the priest at the roman catholic church in our town.

7. She received her masters degree from Florida State University.

8. Survivors include fifteen grandchildren and six great grandchildren.

9. Interment will be in the Greenlawn Cemetary.

10. She lived at 1,200 Westside Rd.

Speeches, News Conferences and Meetings

20

This chapter will give you practice writing the kinds of stories reporters cover frequently. You can choose hard-news or soft approaches, depending on the material. Use your judgment. For access to many online speeches, check the Web site chapter for this book: *http://info.wadsworth.com/rich*.

20-1. Graduation speech

Roger Fidler was director of new media for Knight-Ridder Inc. when he gave the following graduation speech at the University of Colorado. He later became a professor at Kent State University, which is how you can identify him. Fidler became famous for designing a portable flat-panel computer, about the size of an 8- by 10-inch tablet, on which people may receive their newspapers in the future. He is still developing this product. He is considered a leader in the field of innovation in media technology. This is the kind of speech you may frequently have to cover as journalists.

Write this for tomorrow's newspaper, using yesterday as your time frame. You may assume Fidler gave this speech at your college or university. Choose a location on your campus where a graduation ceremony might be held, and figure 2,000 people in the audience or adjust accordingly for your college or university. Try to develop an overall theme to this speech.

I feel truly honored to have been chosen by you to be your commencement speaker. I have spoken at many conferences and to many groups of students and professional journalists in recent years, but this is the first time I've had the privilege of speaking to a graduating class. My hope is that some of what I have to say will be worthy of the honor you have bestowed upon me.

Traditionally, commencement speakers are supposed to rally the spirits of graduating students by painting an exciting picture of their future, and telling them there is no river they can't cross and no mountain they can't scale. I will try to do some of that because I honestly believe the future holds many exciting opportunities, and I still have confidence that any obstacle can be overcome. But, I won't try to fool you.

Your education, until now, has merely provided you with a foundation. Today, your real-life education begins. And I can guarantee you that it will be tougher and more challenging than anything you have experienced so far.

Once the ceremonies have ended and reality sets in, every graduating class has had to face a difficult and often frightening world for which its members have not been fully prepared. That was painfully true for my class and your parents' classes, and it certainly will be true for your class.

Back in the 1960s, when I was a student about to embark on a newspaper career, Bob Dylan told my generation through his music that the times are a changin'. I heard the words, but I had no way of knowing how profoundly social changes and new technologies would transform the news business or of foreseeing the many twists and turns my career would take.

As a young reporter and science writer for the *Eugene Register Guard* in Oregon, I wrote my stories on a manual typewriter in a newsroom that included no women and no minorities. Ten years later I was using a computer terminal to write and edit stories in a newsroom that was no longer an all-white male bastion. Admittedly, diversity still had a long way to go, but it was a start.

During the same brief period, the constant chatter of wire service Teletypes, the pungent smell of molten lead, and the discordant clatter of Linotype machines began giving way to clean and silent digital systems. By the early 1980s, most of the paper and hot-metal production processes that had prevailed for nearly a century were history.

When compared with people in other careers, journalists have always been a somewhat more restless and mobile lot. To be honest, the prospect of traveling and seeing the world actually was one of the prime reasons I chose journalism as a career. I didn't think twice about job hopping if it offered a chance to see new places and develop new skills.

Job hopping is still common among journalists, but the rules have changed in recent years. Until the 1970s, the decision to leave one company and join another was largely in the hands of the employee. Media companies, like most other companies, operated under an unwritten social contract that traded employee loyalty for a guaranteed lifetime job. As a result, most newspaper newsrooms in the 1960s were filled with gray-haired old men wearing green eyeshades and sleeve garters.

All that has changed. The bottom line takes precedent over longevity in a job. It is simply the reality that we must now learn to live with.

Most of you will change jobs far more frequently than those journalists who have preceded you. You will be expected to adapt quickly to technological and operational changes and to continually demonstrate your worth.

Traditional roles are also changing and can be expected to change even faster in the years ahead. Career planning based on contemporary paths and expectations is practically useless. In the 20 years that I was employed by Knight-Ridder, I held nine different positions. What is significant is that none of these positions existed or could have been predicted by a career counselor when I was a student. In most cases, I have actually created my own job and defined the position. This is the future that I believe awaits you.

Changing roles every few years may seem frightening now, but let me assure you that it can be intellectually enriching, as well as financially rewarding. For those of you who want to continue growing and can adapt to change, the future is bright.

While many pundits are predicting that emerging communication technologies will make professional journalists and mass media increasingly irrelevant, I believe, wholeheartedly, that the opposite will be true.

All forms of mass media are undergoing a great transformation brought about by new computer and communication technologies, and a changing media landscape.

But to assume that online databases and interactive televisions will replace traditional media grossly underestimates the resilience and importance of mass media in modern societies.

New technologies will alter existing forms of media and make them more personal and interactive but not eliminate them. I do not believe that technology alone will save or kill traditional media companies. New technologies merely facilitate change and create opportunities.

As the floodgates of the Information Age are opened, I believe the most valued characteristics of mainstream media are likely to be their credibility and connections to the communities they serve.

Learning to create, manage and deliver mixed-media news, advertising, and information on the emerging digital toll roads presents unprecedented challenges for media executives and journalists. To survive, they must adapt to a changing, and often confusing world, where people will have greater personal access to mixed-media information, but will need, even more, the assistance of people they can trust to help them make sense out of it.

For what it is worth, I would like to give you a few predictions of my own about the future that will soon be in your hands.

When media historians a century from now look back on this decade and the first decade of the new millennium, the inventions of this period will be declared at least as significant in the history of human communications systems as the inventions of printing presses and movable type in the last half of the fifteenth century.

I must say that I envy you, because you are among the first generation of post-Industrial Age journalists. You will be the ones who actually transform media and give shape to the future. If history repeats itself, as it always seems to do, digital media and communications may well lead to a global reformation similar in many ways to the Reformation in European societies that followed the invention of the printing press. No one today can predict how society will be transformed.

I am convinced that sometime within the first decade or two of the new millennium, pigmented ink and pulp paper will finally begin to give way to digital ink and silicon paper in the form of portable information appliances.

Within the next two decades we will no longer make distinctions between print and broadcast journalism. The convergence of media technologies will result in the blending of print, video and audio. We will still have different forms of media, but they will not be defined as narrowly as they are today.

No matter which path the future may take, I urge you to take your careers seriously and to become responsible journalists. Avoid at all cost trivializing information and pandering to the lowest common denominators. Be diligent, but be fair, in your roles as watchdogs and guardians of our freedoms. And always remember that the future is what you make of it.

I want to wish all of you a fulfilling life and career. May you all find the joy that comes from doing a job well.

20-2. Vonnegut hoax graduation speech - online

The speech was brilliant, funny and false. Supposedly Kurt Vonnegut had given this graduation speech at MIT in which he urged students to wear sunscreen, floss, dance and do one thing every day that scares you. But it was so clever that the speech was passed around the world via e-mail. Mary Schmich even got a copy of it, and that surprised her. This columnist for the *Chicago Tribune* contacted Vonnegut, who said he was also suprised to learn he had given the speech. He didn't. It was a column Mary Schmich had written for the *Tribune*. You can access the speech and the column through the Web site for this book. If that link is no longer active, do a search for the Kurt Vonnegut graduation speech. It is posted in several sites.

20-3. News Conference

In 1998 Michael Jordan, considered the greatest basketball player in history, retired for the second time -- this time for good, he claimed. He led the Chicago Bulls to six national championships. But his second retirement didn't last more than three years. In 2001 he returned to the court as a player for the Washington Wizards. However, this press conference he gave on his second retirement still serves as a good exercise. For more background information, check the Internet. Here is some brief background:

Michael Jeffrey Jordan led the National Basketball Association league 10 times in scoring. His career average of 31.5 points per game is the best in league history. He helped the Chicago Bulls win six championships. He was 35 when he retired. He has three children. He retired a few years earlier but came back. He is 6 feet 6 inches, and was graduated from the University of North Carolina in 1985. He played for the Chicago Bulls for 13 years. In 1997-98 he was named the NBA's most valuable player for the fifth time. At the press conference, he wore a dark blue suit and a gold earring dangling from his left earlobe. He had a bandage wrapped around his right index finger. He said he had severed a tendon while cutting a cigar. The injury needs surgery and could have kept him from playing for a while but he said he had planned to retire before that.

Here are excerpts from the text of his press conference conducted at the United Center in Chicago. Write a news story based on these remarks as though he made the comments today for tomorrow's newspaper:

Opening comments from Michael Jordan

Well, we do this again for the second time. I was telling my wife coming down, I felt like I was getting married. . . .

My responsibility has been to play the game of basketball and relieve some of the pressure of everyday life for people who work 9 to 5, and I've tried to do that to the best of my abilities.

I am here to announce my retirement from the game of basketball. There won't be another announcement to baseball or anything to that nature. I think everyone has their own reasons. There's been a lot of speculation in terms of why. I'm pretty sure I could get to that point once you guys get to ask questions.

I want to say thank you to both of the gentlemen here. Mr. Stern and Mr. Reinsdorf for presenting me with the opportunity to play the game of basketball and certainly giving me the opportunity to come to Chicago and meet my beautiful wife and build a family here and my family in North Carolina and a lot of my friends who came up here to support this day and who supported me once I stepped on the basketball court and even when I didn't play on the basketball court.

I want to say thanks to both those gentlemen and to all the fans in Chicago for allowing me to come here and they've adopted me to be one of theirs, and in response I've tried to step on the basketball court and get rid of the gangster mentality that Chicago was known for a long time. I think successfully, myself and my teammates and the whole organization has made an effort to change the perspective about Chicago. And we're hopefully going to be known as a championship city.

I hope it continues on even when Michael Jordan is not in uniform. I will support the Chicago Bulls. I think the game itself is a lot bigger than Michael Jordan. I've been given an opportunity by people before me. To name a few: Kareem Abdul-Jabbar, Dr. J, Elgin Baylor, Jerry West, these guys played the game way before Michael Jordan was born. And Michael Jordan came on the heels of all that activity. And Mr. Stern and what he's done for the league and gave me the opportunity to play the game of basketball.

I played it to the best that I could play it. I tried to enhance the game itself. I've tried to be the best basketball player I could be. And next thing you know, here we are as a league. I think the league is going to continue on although we've had our troubles over the last six months. I think that's a reality check for all of us. It is a business but yet it's still fun, it's still a game and the game will continue on.

Once again, I've had a great time. And I can't say enough for the people who've supported me and my life will take a change. And a lot of people say, 'Well, Michael Jordan doesn't have any challenges away from the game of basketball.' Well, I dispute that.

Being a parent is very challenging. If you have kids you know that. I welcome that challenge and I look forward to it.

I will live vicariously through my kids as they play the game of basketball. If they don't, I will support that. My wife and I will do the same. We will do what we can as parents to make sure that happens.

That's the challenge that I have in front of me and I look forward to it. Unfortunately, my mother my family, my brothers and sisters could not be here. But as you see me, you see them.

My father, my mother, and certainly my brothers and sisters, so they are here through me. They along with myself say thank you for taking me in and showing me the respect and certainly the gratitude that you have shown me over the years that I have been here.

I will be in Chicago for my career hopefully and for the rest of my life. My wife won't allow me to move nowhere else. So I will be in Chicago and I will support the Chicago teams. And that's all I really truly have to say. I thought of saying just two words: "I'm gone." But I figured I owe the fans and certainly the media a little bit more than that. So that's one of my reasons for being here.

I guess Jerry wants to speak first before David. I pass it over to Jerry.

Comments from Bulls CEO Jerry Reinsdorf

Well this is a day that I think I hoped would never come. It has to be the toughest day in the history of the Chicago Bulls. It's a tough day for Chicago, it's a tough day for the NBA, it's a tough day for basketball fans all over the world and for Michael Jordan fans all over the world.

Standing here in the United Center where Michael Jordan has given us so many wonderful moments, performances and championships it's hard to imagine games being played here without him.

Michael is simply the best player who ever put on a basketball uniform. He has defined the Bulls, the city and the NBA for more than a decade. He will always represent a standard of excellence.

His statue out in front of the building will greet everybody who ever enters this building again.

When Michael retired in 1993, we retired his No. 23 and hung it in a position of prominence from the rafters. When Michael came back from baseball, he asked me to take it down. He felt funny about playing when his number was hanging up above and so we took it down.

Today, Michael, we are returning your No. 23 to its rightful place of honor, where it will forever serve as a reminder of your dominance on this court and your dominance of this game.

Someday, Michael, the White Sox might retire 45.

And to my leader David Stern, the truth is that for what Michael's meant to the NBA, this number could very well be retired in every arena. Certainly, we in Chicago think that anybody who wears No. 23 with a basketball uniform would look like a pretender.

Finally, Michael, I have one thing to present to you. For the last season, for the last game, for the last shot, I would like to present to you the 1998 World Championship Ring, which certainly means a lot to all of us.

So, Michael, thank you very much for what you have meant to all of the world, there'll never be another one like you.

Comments from NBA commissioner David Stern

Michael, I get to say thank you for 29 teams and hundreds of millions of fans around the world. Thank you for what you've meant to our game, thank you for being who you were, not only for your leadership and greatness on the court, but for who you were and will continue to be off the court.

Your contributions to the NBA are immeasurable, despite the fact that every newspaper in the country has an insert to detail those today and every network has a series of programs to do it. I don't think they could ever capture all that you've meant to us.

Thank you for gracing our court for 13 seasons, and I disagree with Jerry. This is not a sad day. This is a great day, because the greatest basketball player in the history of the game is getting the opportunity to retire with the grace that described his play. So to you and to Juanita and to the challenge that you define of parenthood, I wish you nothing but continued success and hope that you continue to have the good health that goes with it.

Thank you very much.

Questions from the press:

Q. Can you compare the reasons why you retired this time to the reasons why you retired in 1993?

Jordan: Mentally, I am exhausted. I don't feel I have the challenge. The last time in 1993, I had other agendas. I felt that I wanted to play baseball and I felt that at my age, it was a good opportunity and time to do it. . . . I have accomplished everything that I could as an individual.

Q. Is there any chance that you will change your mind?

Jordan: No, I never say never, but 99.9 percent I am very secure with my decision.

Q. Why do you have to walk out of here with that one percent in your pocket?

Jordan: Because it is my one percent and not yours. That's why.

For more information, search the NBA Web site:
http://nba.com/

20-4. Meeting advance

The story you write before the meeting about issues the governmental body will discuss is often more important than the actual meeting story. The meeting advance informs readers so they have a chance to express their views at the meeting. You should get a copy of the meeting agenda a few days before the meeting. Write a meeting advance based on the following information:

You have received an agenda of the city commission meeting in your community. (Substitute commission for council or whatever your local city government body is called.) Read the following agenda and decide what item or items you think are worthy of an advance story. Here are some of the items on the agenda:

A. Consent agenda: All matters listed on the consent agenda are considered under one motion and will be enacted by one motion. There will be no separate discussion of those items. If discussion is desired, that item will be removed from the consent agenda and considered separately.

  1. Review and approve minutes of various boards and commissions:
          City Commission meeting of previous week.
          Aviation Advisory Board meeting of previous week.
  2. Approve renewal of the following licenses:
          a. Drinking establishments: Barb Wire's Steak House & Saloon, 2412 Iowa;
  3. Bid item:
          a. Set bid date of Jan. 5 for annual lubricants contract (Public Works)
  4. Approve on second and final reading, the following ordinances
          a. Ordinance No. 6354 annexing a 28.5 acre tract of land generally
located south of Sixth Street and west of Wakarusa Drive.
          5. Ordinance No. 6395 authorizing the issuance of $6,000,000 multi-family housing development revenue refunding bonds for Brandon Woods nursing home, 15th and Inverness Drive. (Approved by the commission on [date specified].

B. Consider the following regular agenda items:
          1. Conduct a public hearing and consider adopting Resolution No. 5501 declaring house at 1222 Summit St. blighted.
                  Action: Adopt Resolution No. 5501 if appropriate.
          2. Consider proposed request for proposals for architectural consultant services related to proposed renovation and expansion of city art center.
                  Action: Authorize request for proposals.
          3. Receive feasibility update report from consulting team about building a public golf course.
                  Action: Receive and discuss study
          4. Receive staff report and draft ordinance prohibiting nudity in establishments selling intoxicating liquors.
                  Action: Receive staff† report, direct placement of ordinance on next
          5. Consider approval of contract with Hamm Quarry Inc. for landfill services.
          6. Consider appointments to various boards.

You have reviewed the agenda and have decided to focus on the proposed ordinance banning nudity or the consultants' report on the proposed city golf course. You call some of the commissioners (there are five) and find out they are really concerned about nudity in the local bars. City Manager Mike Wildgen tells you the concern was fostered because they received a proposal from a man who wants to start a bar featuring topless female dancers. The manager and commissioners don't tell you who he is, but they say they want to create an ordinance preventing nudity in bars or other establishments that serve liquor just to prevent someone from setting up such a place. Currently no bars in your city feature nude dancers.

Background:

The proposed ordinance would affect only businesses licensed to sell alcohol. It would not affect other "adult entertainment" establishments such as X-rated movie theaters. The proposed ordinance says: "Alcohol-licensed establishments that offer nude dancing foster and promote incidents of criminal activity, can and do adversely affect property values, can and do contribute to neighborhood decay and blight, and do create direct exposures to health risks and potential health hazards."

Johnson County, a neighboring county, is being sued by a club and several nude dancers who say that the county's ban on nude dancing is unconstitutional.

Here are some of the commissioners' comments:

Commissioner Bob Walters: "I'm not a prude. But I don't think that nude entertainment in any form should be allowed in any business with access to the public. Sometimes I don't understand why we can't do what we think is in the best interests of the community."

Commissioner Bob Schumm: "We just don't need it (nudity). We're doing fine without it. This is a wholesome city, a good place to raise a family and we don't need all the problems that go along with (adult entertainment)."

Commissioner Shirley Martin-Smith: "I am not into banning free speech or banning anything, but I am into putting some controls on entertainment that is not a benefit to the community. People are just amazed that this even needs to be an issue. I think the point of the ordinance is to eliminate the possibility of nudity as entertainment in the city. I think we just have to pursue it and see where it takes us, which is what we do on a lot of issues."

County Chief Deputy Counselor, LeeAnne Gillaspie: The legal basis for restricting behavior in such clubs was firmly stated in the 21st Amendment to the Constitution, which outlawed Prohibition and gave states the power to restrict alcohol consumption. She said once the law moves away from alcohol (such as regulating juice bars, for example), the issue moves into the First Amendment and freedom of expression guarantees.

The meeting will be conducted at 6:30 p.m. Monday in your city hall (give the address) or use Sixth and Massachusetts streets.

Based on a story from the *Lawrence* (Kan.) *Daily Journal-World.* Used with permission.

20-5. Meeting story

Write a story based on the following information from a city council meeting:

The City Council (five members including the mayor and vice mayor) in your town is conducting its regular weekly meeting. Several items are on the agenda. They include:

Consent agenda:

Approve minutes of the last meeting.

Consider spending $44,000 for two vans and a four-wheel drive pickup for use by the city's maintenance personnel.

Receive an annual audit report from the accounting firm of Schehrer, Harrod and Bennett.

Other items:

Consider cutting five positions from the police department and consolidating some police support services with the county for a savings of $762,301.

Consider a recommendation from the planning commission to rezone 34 acres of agricultural land in the western part of the city to residential use.

Consider revising an ordinance prohibiting potbellied pigs.

The meeting was called to order at 8 a.m. A motion was made to approve the consent agenda. It was unanimously approved.

Vice Mayor Charles Shorter moved to cut five positions from the police department. Police Chief Samuel Safety strenuously objected. He said the cuts would hamper his department's ability to patrol the streets. He said the loss of police officers is coming at a time when the crime rate is increasing. Shorter said the city had to reduce spending somewhere, and by consolidating some other services with the county, the Police Department could cut the positions from its administrative and clerical staff. "I am not recommending that the reductions be made to the police force," Shorter said. The motion was approved unanimously.

Commissioner Shirley Wise moved to accept the recommendation of the Planning Commission. The motion was unanimously approved.

Shorter moved to reconsider an ordinance the council passed last week outlawing swine in city limits. He said a pig owner had caused him to reconsider.

Mayor David Fischer asked if any members of the public wished to speak to the issue.

Janie Finck, the owner of a Vietnamese potbellied pig, requested to speak. She brought her pet with her. She said her pig is named Bo Jackswine, in honor of athlete Bo Jackson. Finck was wearing pig emblem earrings as she showed her 42-

114

pound pig to the council members. Finck had the pig sit up for a treat. After seeing the pig, several council members expressed their support and engaged in pig puns.

The pig wore a red bow around his neck. He swished his tail constantly and walked to the end of his leash to sniff people curiously.

Councilman Robert Stewart said: "Let me mention that Bo Jackswine has been a constituent of mine for over a year and there have been no complaints. He's a perfect neighbor."

Shorter said he was so impressed by the pig that he might consider getting one himself.

"Talk about rolling over," Fischer quipped. "All right, let's have a swine call."

The council voted unanimously to ask the city attorney to rework city laws to reclassify Vietnamese potbellied pigs as domestic animals. That would make it legal to keep them within city limits.

Finck told council members: "Thank you very much. Bo thanks you very much. I am very happy. And Bo did excellent. He was definitely a ham."

After the vote you get these reactions from the people who came to urge council to change the ordinance so they could keep their potbellied pigs.

From John Hood, who owns a white Vietnamese potbellied pig named Gidget: He said his pig means the world to him. "It was either they pass it or I'd have moved out. You can steal my truck or anything else, but you better leave my pig alone."

From Kris Guidice, owner of Popeye and Ryne, two Vietnamese potbellied pigs: "I took off work. I haven't slept in two days because I've been so worried about it."

The council will conduct a public hearing and consider final approval of the revised ordinance at 8 a.m. on May 7 at City Hall.

The pig ordinance information is adapted from a story in the *St. Petersburg* (Fla.)*Times.* Used with permission.

20-6. School board meeting

Read the following script of a school board meeting and write a story, choosing the most interesting item for your focus.

The Rockville School Board is conducting its weekly meeting at 7 p.m. in the school administration building, at 2500 Addison Place. (You may substitute the name of the school board in your town for this exercise.) Write a story based on the scenario that follows.

School board members are as follows: Alfred C. Robertson (president), William Harold, Maria Santana, Peter Bodine (Board secretary), Denise Davis. The meeting begins with a motion to approve the minutes of the last meeting, and the board unanimously approves.

Robertson: Next item on the agenda is to receive bids for three new school buses.

Bodine: We've got kind of a deal here. One bus company, Sierra Busing, has entered a bid of $23,520. Now that's for a normal bus that can hold 84 students. Another company, Buses Unlimited, offers an 84-seater that runs on diesel for $24,000 even. The Springfield Valley Unified School District has offered one of their used buses for $12,000. Again it holds 84 people, but it's got 80,000 miles on it and is a '78 model.

Davis: Is 80,000 too many?

Bodine: No, I don't think so. I'd recommend that bus.

Santana: Why are they selling it?

Bodine: The district is growing smaller and they don't need it. And they're in a budget crunch.

Davis: But why this particular one? Something wrong with it?

Bodine: No. Our district's mechanic checked it out and said it's fine. Purrs like a kitten were his exact, if unoriginal, words.

Davis: I move we accept the bid of $12,000 from the Springfield Valley Unified School District for the offered bus.

Robertson: Do I hear a second.

Harold: Second.

Robertson: All in favor say aye. (Board unanimously approves.)

Robertson: Next item on the agenda is the appropriation of funds to put the basketball team up in a hotel for three days. The high school's team won the division tournament and is going to the state finals in Phoenix. If they continue their winning ways, they will have to stay up there at least three days. The appropriation requests $125 per night so the basketball team can compete in state playoffs for as long as they need to stay in Phoenix.
(The motion is seconded, and the board unanimously approves.)

Robertson: The next request is from the high school librarian for money. Mr. Secretary, will you please read the request?

Bodine: I have a request here from Mrs. Phyllis Laird, head librarian. It reads: "In order to keep our library in tune with modern times, update reference materials, replace damaged and lost books, and add new magazines to our subscription list, we are asking for $543 before the next school year. A well-stocked library is a necessary part of a student's education, and so I hope you will grant our request." Mrs. Laird goes on to list how the money would be spent.

Robertson: For a set of new encyclopedias to replace our 1975 versions, a new set of science-oriented encyclopedias, magazine subscriptions to *Time, Newsweek, Sports Illustrated, Boys Life* and something called *Dragon.* I don't know what that is for sure. Then she's got an almanac and other reference materials and about 200 books. You all have read the lists, right?

All: Nod and mumble in the affirmative.

Robertson: What do you think of Mrs. Laird's choices?

Harold: I have no problems with the request, and I move we vote to authorize the appropriation for $543 for the school library.

Robertson: Well, before we take a second on your motion, I think we ought to discuss these books and magazines a little.

Harold: What's to discuss? They're all fine books.

Bodine: I'm not so sure I want to agree to this authorization. Some of these books, I think, are questionable. I have no objections to Shakespeare or even books like *Megatrends* or Lee Iacocca's autobiography. But some of these bother me. As an example I give this one – Kurt Vonnegut's book, *Slaughterhouse Five.* There are some sections in here that deal with sex, others put down the United States. It's strange fare and I'm not so sure Rockville kids need to read stuff like that.

Robertson: Well, I had some reservations on some of these myself, Mr. Bodine. I've heard that this *Catcher in the Rye* by J.D. Salinger, down near the bottom of the list, is about homosexuality. I don't think our students ought to be educated about such topics.

Harold: Mr. President, am I to assume you don't want to approve the request for money because of some of the books on the list?

Robertson: No, Mr. Harold. I'm willing to approve the request, just minus some of the books and magazines.

Harold: That sounds like censorship to me.

Bodine: I think it's censorship, Bill, but it's good censorship. We're concerned for these children, and I think that some of these books can only hinder a student's development. We should be careful here. Would you want students to read a book that perpetuates racial stereotypes? Have you ever read *Huckleberry Finn?* That novel just reeks with the degradation of blacks.

Robertson: I don't even think we need to look at some of them. Students don't need to read trash. Though, I wonder what you've got against Huck Finn. I read it as a boy, and I think it's a fine novel.

Santana: I think I agree with Mr. Bodine. I try to watch my kids. I've read reports in newspapers about kids who read comic books or those sword and sorcery books and then go out and play Dungeons and Dragons and then end up committing suicide. Maybe we should look at these things.

Harold: Maria, do you monitor what your kids watch on TV?

Santana: No, not really.

Harold: So you let your kids watch something where people run around shooting 1,000 rounds of ammunition per show. Now, do your kids run out and grab machine guns and start shooting each other? No, so why would books have that effect?

Bodine: I think it's the potential for that effect. A student who is violent or depressed may be pushed over the edge.

Harold: You can't protect them from everything. And in the meantime, they could lose something valuable. It's important that a child reads, and I don't care if the kid reads cigarette packages or *War and Peace.* The important thing is that they are learning how words work and how to communicate.

Bodine: OK, then, why don't we put *Playboy* in the library? So long as reading is the only thing that's important.

Harold: Get serious, Peter. You know I'm not advocating that.

Bodine: So you will censor, just to a different degree.

Davis: I've been sitting here watching you debate. Twenty-five years ago we had this same type of discussion. But back then we were talking about John Steinbeck. A number of parents were concerned that the subject matter in *The Grapes of Wrath* would be too shocking to students. They believed it portrayed a world and an attitude of negativism and pessimism. A book is neither good or bad. It all depends on how it is used and read. I would give students the option. Open our library to different books and let them decide. I don't believe it is our place to dictate what a student can and cannot read.

Santana: Well, are we going to vote on something? Should have a new motion.

Bodine: I move we set a public hearing two weeks from today to get parents' reactions to these books.

Santana: I second the motion.

Harold: Mr. President, I wonder exactly what that will accomplish. We have over 200 books on this list. I doubt that the public has read all of them. I doubt we've read all of them. You're still talking as if you intend to censor if parents say it's all right with them. Are we each going to vote on 200 books? Where do you start and stop?

Davis: I agree with Bill. Even if we decide that the board has the power to censor, I believe it would be too difficult to decide what should be censored. And that is the strongest argument for not censoring. The world is out there, good and bad. We can't stop it from touching the children. Teach them what's good and bad and use those books as examples. But don't close their minds.

Robertson: We have a motion on the floor to schedule a public hearing regarding the book list Mrs. Laird has submitted. I'd like a roll call vote. How do you vote?

Davis: No.

Harold: No.

Santana: Yes.

Bodine: Yes.

Robertson: Aye. The ayes have it. By a vote of 3-2 a public hearing will be scheduled for Friday, April 18, at 7 p.m. here to discuss the book list and appropriation request.

Member of the audience: You're all nuts. I'll be back here in two weeks to tell you that. I can't believe you're so damn foolish.

Harold: (addressing the audience member) I believe they're that foolish. I'll vote against every stupid goddam thing you propose.

Robertson: Do we have a motion to close this meeting?

Santana: So moved.

The board seconded and approved the motion, and the meeting was adjourned.

This script was adapted from one written by journalism students at the University of Arizona.

20-7. Style quiz

Correct the spelling and style errors in the following sentences.

1. The board voted three to two to have a public hearing about banning some books from the library.

2. The Lawrence city commission will discuss an ordinance to bann nudity from bars or restaurants that serve alchohol.

3. Mike Wildgen, City Manager, said the proposed law would only effect busineses that serve liquor.

4. The first amendment to the constitution guaranties the right to freedom of expression so the proposed ordinence can not be applied to places that don't serve alcohol, said the county's Chief deputy counselor.

5. Vice mayor Charles Shorter was so impressed by the pig that he said he might consider getting one himself.

6. The issue of banning pigs was discussed by the St. Petersburg city council.

7. One woman brought her potbellied pig to city hall when the council debated the ordinence.

8. Earvin Magic Johnson had a garanteed contract for $3,100,000 dollars.

9. Burl Osborne is very concerned about preserving the Constitutional guarantees of free speech.

10. Osborne said that many colleges had adopted speech codes in the 1990's.

Government
and Statistical Stories

21

This chapter will give you practice writing stories with statistics and will test your understanding of terms in government budget stories. The online resources for federal and state governmental information and statistics abound. You can tailor many of these exercises to your own community by clicking into the resources listed on the Web site for this book: *http://info.wadsworth.com/rich.*

To figure percentage changes, subtract the previous year's figure from the current or most recent figure and divide the difference by the previous year's figure.

21-1. Government and weather terms test

Circle the correct answer in the following multiple-choice questions. In some cases more than one answer is correct. For weather terms, check your *Associated Press Stylebook.*

1. A fiscal year is
   a. the year in which a city saves money.
   b. the year the city issues a rate for bonds.
   c. the year for which a budget applies.

2. An operating budget is
   a. the one a city uses to pay for major improvements.
   b. the one a city uses to pay for most services, such as police, fire and salaries.
   c. the one a city uses to pay for state-financed road operations.

3. When a city or state conducts reappraisal, it means
   a. it reorganizes its government operations.
   b. it reevaluates the way cities levy taxes.
   c. it reevaluates property values.

4. A mill is

    a. one tenth of a cent.

    b. $1 for every $1,000 that a property is assessed.

    c. a unit often used for tax rates.

5. A deficit is

    a. leftover money in the budget.

    b. a debt.

    c. a lack of revenue to meet the budget.

6. A capital budget is

    a. a really good budget year

    b. a budget for major expenses usually financed by bonds

    c. a budget of revenues

7. Revenues in a budget are

    a. leftover funds.

    b. the income in a budget.

    c. the remaining money after the budget is proposed.

8. A hurricane is a storm in which sustained winds

    a. must be at least 45 mph.

    b. must be over 74 mph.

    c. must be over 95 mph.

9. To qualify as a blizzard, a snowstorm must have wind speeds of at least

    a. 50 mph.

    b. 35 mph.

    c. 25 mph.

10. The wind chill factor is

    a. the combined effect of wind and cold temperatures on exposed skin.

    b. the combined effect of wind and cold temperatures in the atmosphere.

    c. the combined effect of wind and cold temperatures compared to the previous year.

21-2. Statistics – crime rates

Assume that these are the annual crime rate statistics for your state, released by your state Bureau of Investigation. Decide which are the most dramatic findings to report. Using the statistics and information from sources, write a news story. Do not flood your lead with statistics. Analyze the most interesting information and write a summary lead based on that. You don't need all the statistics in your story, but you should include the most important ones. Your story will be accompanied by a graphic.

Type	Last year	This year	Percent change
Murder	138	204	47.8
Forcible rape	1,518	1,584	4.3
Robbery	2,982	3,637	22
Aggravated assault	12,673	13,429	6
Burglary	39,626	38,869	-1.9
Larceny/theft	127,336	131,305	3.1
Motor vehicle theft	14,094	14,346	1.8
Total	198,367	203,364	2.5

Other statistics from your State Bureau of Investigation:
Based on statistics for the current year, bureau officials say that in your state:
☛ Someone becomes a victim of violent crime every 30 minutes.
☛ An assault is committed (in your state) every 41 minutes.
☛ A rape is committed every 5 hours and 46 minutes.
☛ A murder is committed every 63 hours.

Comments from sources:
From Mike Stiers, division chief of the bureau: "The increase in violence is what really concerns us. They're either bashing them in the head or shooting them when it's not necessary. The increase in violent crime reflects a greater social problem that can't be solved by police alone. We're losing the battle here. People need to realize this. They need to demand of their legislators, both state and municipal, that they don't want to live like this."

From Julie Reaman, a therapist with Ending the Violence Effectively, a counseling group for victims: Increased publicity about sexual assault and incest may have boosted the reporting rate.

From Anne Byrne of the Rape Awareness and Assistance Program: "I don't think it's a huge increase in the amount of reports. I think more sexual assaults are going on. I don't know why; it's alarming."

From Bob Allen, county undersheriff: "I think it has to do with a general downward trend in morality, a breakdown in family. That's a community function, everybody pulling together and starting to work together. Many murders are committed by family or acquaintances. I personally feel that people who do it are people who know each other. That's typical of homicide. You always hurt the one you love."

Based on a story from the *Rocky Mountain News*. Used with permission.

21-3. Weather statistics

Was it the hottest or coldest season, the wettest or driest? People like to read about weather. So reporters periodically have to write weather stories summarizing the statistics for the month, the season or the year. Here are some annual statistics – minus December – for three counties in South Florida, where weather is important news. Compare the statistics and find an angle for your story.

The following statistics compare rainfall levels (in inches) for the months with normal rainfall. Months are divided into the normally wet and dry seasons for Broward, Palm Beach, and Dade counties. You are writing this story in November as a weather roundup for that month for a newspaper that serves these three counties. Assume you are writing this for the current year. This chart will run with your story. The only comment you have is from Geoff Shaughnessy, meteorologist for the South Florida Water Management District, who said the rain in November came from moisture-laden weather fronts that stalled over South Florida, a phenomenon that is more typical for October. Write a very brief story, approximately six to eight inches, or about a page and a half of double-spaced typed copy. Assume that you have a weather forecast of a new front coming through that is expected to bring more rain.

Dry	Broward	Palm Beach	Dade	Norm
Jan.	2.88	1.89	2.15	2.41
Feb.	2.49	3.86	1.64	2.19
March	1.97	2	3.01	2.7
April	3.63	3.05	2.75	3.43
Wet				
May	0.94	1.1	0.81	5.87
June	16.84	16.45	20.95	8.1
July	3.35	2.91	3.5	6.41
Aug.	8.4	8.38	11.41	6.83
Sept.	3.81	6.81	4.07	8.52
Oct.	1.88	1.27	1.63	7.84
Dry				
Nov.	6.91	11.14	6.41	2.84
Dec.	——	——	——	2.02
Total	53.09	58.86	58.33	59.16

21-4. City budget story

Your city commission (or whatever your local governing body is called) is considering a proposed budget for the coming year. The budget was presented to the commission yesterday by the city manager. Read the following budget information and analyze where expenditures increased or decreased the most. Decide what kinds of questions you might ask the city manager. Look at the tax rate (the mill levy) and decide if it has increased, decreased or stayed the same. Then, using the chart on how to figure your taxes, explain in your story what that rate will mean for the owner of a home assessed at $15,000, an average assessment in your community. The city assesses homes at 15 percent of market value, so a home worth $100,000 would be assessed at $15,000 for tax purposes. Use an impact lead telling readers what this budget means to them and explaining how their money will be spent. Comments from the manager follow.

General operating budget – summary of expenditures

Item	Last year	Current Year	Proposed next year
Public works	573,089	784,700	864,000
Water/sewage	9,117,586	10,360	10,977,027
Parks/recreation	634,945	697,400	810,800
Business improvement	0	0	83,689
Employee benefits	3,102,708	3,446,800	3,380,450
Bonds/interest	3,643,654	3,125,413	4,252,000
Sanitation	2,241,201	2,641,200	2,949,540
Police	2,881,738	3,101,800	3,197,350
Fire	132,722	2,191,750	23,433,050
Animal control	581,390	128,550	**130,120**
Library	581,390	662,180	723,913
General operations	6,554,490	7,227,339	6,927,180
Total	31,478,139	34,366,890	36,639,119
	42.2	42	42.2

Revenues: About 57% of revenues come from property taxes. Other sources include $15,805,749 from various taxes such as:

Property tax	$ 20,833,370
Gas taxes	$ 1,089,440
Alcohol	$ 230,133
Guest tax	$ 185,000
Water/sewer	$ 10,977,027
Sanitation	$ 2,949,540
Fed. revenue sharing	$ 25,000
Parking meters	$ 265,920
Business improvements	$ 83,689
Total	**$ 36,639,119**

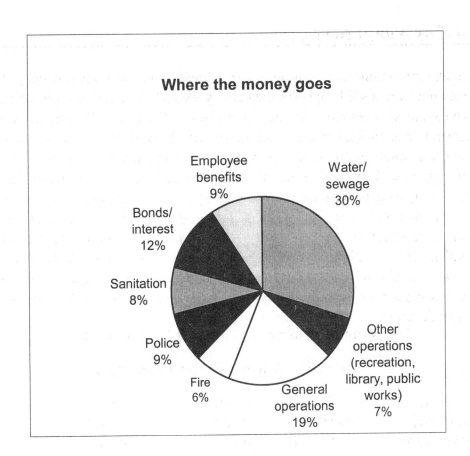

Where the money goes

- Employee benefits 9%
- Water/sewage 30%
- Bonds/interest 12%
- Sanitation 8%
- Police 9%
- Fire 6%
- General operations 19%
- Other operations (recreation, library, public works) 7%

How to figure your property tax

1. Write the assessed value of your property in Box A. This is the amount your property is appraised for   tax purposes, not the amount of money it would sell for on the market. For example, if you have a   house worth $100,000 and the city assesses it at 15% of its value for taxes, your assessed value is $15,000.
2. Divide the figure in Box A by 1,000 because a mill is $1 tax on every $1,000 of assessed value. Write the result in Box B.
3. Write the mill levy in Box C. For this city, the levy proposed is 42.2 mills.
4. . Multiply the figures in Boxes B and C. Write the result in Box D. This is the amount of taxes you will owe to the city.

Calculate your tax rate

Assessed value: **A**

Divided by 1,000: **B**

Mill levy: **C**

Multiply B X C =Taxes:
          D

Remarks by City Manager Michael A. Thrifty

I am hereby submitting the recommended budget for the coming fiscal year commencing in July. The current fiscal budget is presented as a working document for your consideration. (City commissioners must conduct public hearings before they can adopt it. Public hearings will be scheduled at the end of the month.)

The proposed budget totals $36,639,119 as compared to the current budget of $34,366,890. The proposed budget is presented to you with a minimal increase in the tax rate of 42.20 mills or $42.20 per $1,000 of assessed valuation, compared to 42.10 mills for the current year. We have estimated the assessed valuation at the time of budget preparation to be $493,681,760. The real estate valuation has grown $5,100,000 in the past year, which will provide us with more revenue from property taxes without raising taxes. The budget concentrates on providing current staff levels. However, the growth we are experiencing places pressure on current staffing levels in public safety, public works and parks maintenance.

Our bond indebtedness continues to increase. Part of that is due to a $1 million bond issue voters approved in the last election to fund a new recreation center. Providing water and sewage treatment for our growing population continues to be a significant portion of our budget.

Specific recommendations in this budget are as follows:

- A 3% salary increase for all employees
- The amount of refuse collected, number of customers added and size of area serviced for the Sanitation Department has significantly increased in the past five years. I am recommending addition of one residential crew supervisor, one commercial crew supervisor, two commercial drivers, and two commercial loaders. Two years ago city crews collected 34,018 tons of refuse; last year it was 41,357 tons and to date the rate will result in 44,734 tons.
- Two of the downtown parking lots will be overlaid with asphalt this summer, and I am recommending $25,000 be allocated in the parking meter fund to continue the maintenance program.
- The Business Improvement District is included for the first time. The income from this district with a 1 percent tax for improvement of the downtown business area will be the revenue source.

> Respectfully submitted,
> City Manager Michael A. Thrifty

(In addition to city taxes, residents pay county and school taxes, but those taxes are levied in separate budgets by the school district and the county. The total tax rate last year for city, county and school taxes was 127 mills.)

21-5. Online statistical profile of a community

Write a statistical profile story about a neighborhood in your community. Use the Wall Street Journal formula of focusing on a person before you launch into statistics. For example, interview one or two of your classmates; get their ZIP codes. Then write "She/He is one of ....) and describe the community. An easy way to do this is to click into community demographic data on the Web site for this book or link directly to the CACI marketing site, which offers data for communities by ZIP codes. Access it at: *http://www.demographics.caci.com/free_samples/zip_code_searches.htm.* Type in a few adjacent ZIP codes and write a comparative statistical profile of several communities in your city or adjacent cities.

21-6. Caffeine consumption

How much caffeine are you consuming? If you are drinking herbal tea to cut down on your coffee consumption, you might be getting almost as much caffeine in your ginseng tea. If you eat Ben & Jerry's coffee yogurt ice cream, you could get almost as much caffeine as by drinking coffee. Is caffeine dangerous? Write a story about caffeine by using statistics and press releases from the Center for Science in the Public Interest. You can supplement your statistics with interviews of your classmates and friends about their favorite drinks, drugs (Excedrin and the like) and candy. If the caffeine statistics are no longer available, check the Web site for other reports containing statistics. You can access the CPSI caffeine chart on the center's site at: *http://www.cspinet.org/new/cafchart.htm*

21-7. Style quiz

1. The tax rate of 42 mills means residents will pay $42 for every $100 that their property is assessed.

2. Crime rose 2 and a half % and robberies increased 21.6 percent.

3. Broward County's 6.91 in. of Nov. rain was more than 2 times the normal amount.

4. A 12 member commitee headed by the City Manager reccomended that the tax rate be kept at it's current level.

5. Taxpayers will pay $42.20 for every $1000 of asessed value on there property.

6. The budget was recommended by city manager Michael A. Thrifty.

7. A mill is equal to $100 for every one thousand dollars of assessed property value.

8. The university is coping with a $6.100,000 million dollar shortfall.

9. The weather forecast calls for more rain in Palm Beach county and winds up to 30 miles per hour.

10. The bill being debated by the Colorado house judiciary committee is similar to ones proposed in Legislatures in other states.

Crime and Punishment

22

This chapter will give you practice writing crime and court stories. You must be careful to attribute all accusatory information. The stories are geared to a variety of writing techniques, but you should exercise good judgment before writing a soft lead or using a lighthearted tone. You'll find many online resources for crime statistics from your campus or community police department and official court records online. You can access them from the book Web site: *http://info.wadsworth.com/rich*.

22-1 a–b. Police reports

Assume that you are a police reporter and you check the police reports every day. You conduct interviews for major crime stories and write briefs from the reports for all accidents and other incidents. Police forms vary from one agency to another, but all forms will contain some of the basic information included in the following ones. Write briefs for each one of these reports, attributing your information to police reports. You decide if the physical description of the victims and offenders is necessary. You may substitute your city for the cities in the reports. Use delayed identification leads for each of your stories.

22a. Motor vehicle accident

Motor Vehicle Accident Report

(Check one) Fatal √ Injury Hit/run	√ Property Damage under $500	Property Damage over $500
Milepost County Hwy/Road/ Street & Speed limit 13 St. and Missouri Ave. 35 mph	City/Town/State Your town, Your state	Local case no. 1395696
Distance ft./mi.& Dir.from/at hwy/road/street 10 ft. from 13th St. at Missouri St. intersection	Investigating Dept. Investigating Officer Your P.D. Ron Williams	Reviewed by Lt. J. Mullens

Collision diagram (Show unit movements, roads)		
North Veh. 2 ⇓ **Missouri** ⇓ ⇓ 13th ---------------------------------- ⇓ ---------- **13th St.** Veh. I ⇒ ⇒ ⇒ ⇒ ⇒ **X** **West** **East** **South**	Describe pre-crash movement or action and direction of vehicles and pedestrians/cyclists Operator of Veh. #1 was driving east on 13th when Veh. 2 going south on Missouri failed to yield right of way and collided with it.	Date of accident Use today's date Time 0800 Time arrived/& Day 0804 Today's date

Veh. 1. left front door dented, windshield cracked Veh. 2, fender dented
Name/address of object owner: Doolittle, Brenda; 1225
Pennsylvania Ave., Your town, Your state.

Unit Driver/Pedes. Name, last, first & initial Phone 1 Doolittle, Brenda M. 555-1442	Color Year & make of vehicle Model & body style Blue 1996 Ford Escort hatchback	
Driver/pedes. address (Number, street, city, state, zip code) 1225 Pennsylvania Ave., Your town	State License Plate Your state HV 623	Removed by: Owner
Driver's license state and number Date of birth Sex 1315121212 1 1/30/66 F	Vehicle Identification no. F 1223456666	Odometer 25,678
Registered owner full name ("Same" if driver) Phone Same	Total no. of vehicle occupants including driver 1	Insurance Allstate- 12345678
Owner Address ("Same" if driver) Same		
Special conditions (if any) for unit above **none** l. hit/run	2. Non-contact 3. Stolen 4. Parked 5. Police pursuit 6. Driverless	
Unit Driver/Pedes. Name, last, first & initial Phone 2 Collier, Scott D. 555-54M	Color Year & make of vehicle Model & body style White 1995 Honda Civic sedan	
Driver/ped address (Number, street, city, state, zip code) 1234 Green Street, Your town, state and ZIP	State License Plate Your state FOI-999	Removed by: owner
Driver's license state and number Date of birth Sex 9976543212 11/01/78 M	Vehicle Identification no. 9976543777	Odometer 32,000
Registered owner full name (Same if driver) Phone Same	Total no. of vehicle occupants including driver 1	Insurance Co./policy Allied 76W21
Owner Address ("Same" if driver) same		
Special conditions (if any) for unit above **none** 1.hit/run	2. Non-contact 3. Stolen 4. Parked 5. Police pursuit 6. Driverless	

Record all injured and uninjured occupants and pedestrians   (Use supplemental page if necessary.)

Unit	Last name First initial	Address	Sex	Seatbelt	Eject	Trap	Injury	EMS unit
Unit			F	N	N	N	bruises	N
1	**Doolittle**, Brenda M.	1225 Pennsylvania Ave. Your town, your state						

EMS unit none injured taken by: herself	Taken to: Memorial Hospital

- - -

Dr./pd # Violation charged Citation No.   Operator I - Cit. No. 33393 Failure to wear seatbelt
                                     Op. 2, Ch. 44493 Failure to yield right of way

22b. Burglary

1. Dispatched 1 2. Citizen 3. On view	Name of agency Your town P.D.	Case No. 1395893	Date of Offense Use yesterday	Time 0100	Date of Report Yesterday, this year
Location of offense 515 SE Mission St.	Time reported 0100	Time arrived 0105	Time cleared 0330		

Offense-List most serious first A. Attempted Burglary (felony) B Criminal damage to property (misdemeanor)	Type of premise: (List no.) 4 　1. Street 　2. Single residence 　3. Multiple residence 　4. Commercial 　5. Gas station 　6. Convenience store 　7. Pharmacy/doctor office 　8. Public community bldg	9. Restaurant 10. Storage/ warehouse 11. Tavern/bar/liquor 12. Vehicle 13. Bank 14. Open area (park, field) 15. Other

Codes: 0	V = Victim	0 = Offender	W = Witness	RP = Reporting Party	

Type: (Use no.) 1
1. Individual	3.Society/public	5.Religious organization	7.Other
2.Business	4.Financial Institution	6. Government	8.Unknown

Name: Last First Middle Code
Stanton Joseph 0,

Address: Street city &late Homeless						Zip
Telephone No. (Home) Race Caucasian	Sex Res/non. Res. M　　R	Date of Birth 1/10/72	Height 6'2	Weight 210	Hair brown	Eyes brown

Codes:	V = Victim	O = Offender	W = Witness	RP = Reporting Party	

Type: (Use code.) V 2/5
1. Individual	3.Society/public	5.Religious organization	7.Other
2. Business	4.Financial Institution	6. Government	8.Unknown

Name: Last　First　Middle　　　Code V
　　Salvation Army

Address: Street city State 515 SE Mission, Your city, Your state				Zip Yours
Telephone No. (Home Race Sex Res/non. Res. 555-0987	Age	Date of birth		Height Weight Hair Eyes

Describe briefly how offense was committed.
Officer Dean Williams and myself responded to an alarm at the Salvation Army building at 0100. When we arrived, we saw a man running from the building. Williams gave chase and caught perpetrator. Mr. Stanton informed us that he had broken into the building in search of food. He said, "I was trying to find some food and I had no place to stay." Mr. Stanton has no known address. He was taken to the County Jail. Charged with attempted burglary, criminal damage to property.

Property Description 4
Type property loss 1 =None　　2 =Burned　　3-=Counterfeited/forgery
4 =Destroyed/damaged/vandalized　　5 = Recovered　　6 = Stolen　　7 = Unknown

Type: loss	Description	Quantity	Value	Date Recovered	Property total
Window on east side of building broken. No indication of food or other items missing.					

Reporting Officer Off. Ed Kellerman	Badge ID 03567	Date Today's date; this year	Typed by: CKR

22-2. Hourglass Burglary

Write this story in hourglass form. Be careful to attribute any accusatory statements to the police. You may try a creative lead because there were no fatalities or injuries.

You call the local sheriff's department. A spokesman for the Pasco Sheriff's Department [or your county's department], Jon Powers, tells you that five boys, one 11, one 14 and three age 15, were arrested yesterday. He says he cannot release their names because they are juveniles. He said the boys have all been charged with burglary to a vehicle. He says they all admitted to the crime.

You ask for details and he tells you that they were charged with breaking into a food supply truck with a crowbar and stealing assorted boxes of candy, cookies and snacks. He says the goods were worth more than $500. Powers gives you this scenario: The stealing started late last night when two of the boys, who are brothers, saw the truck in the parking lot. The older brother, 15, took a crowbar from a neighbor's yard and pried the padlock off the truck's rear door. He and his brother, 11, then took a carton of candy from the truck. They later told the other boys what they had done.

Powers says the boys tried to carry the goodies home, but the boxes became too heavy for them. They left a 50-pound box of Milky Ways on a bench in front of a Winn Dixie supermarket (according to the police report). You ask what other kinds of candy and snacks they took. Powers says the stolen material included the case of Milky Way bars, boxes of cheese crackers and popcorn and a carton of chocolate creme-filled cookies. You ask what kind of truck it was. He says the truck was Lance Inc. food truck that was in a parking lot on Darlington Road. Lance supplies food for vending machines.

Based on a story from the *St. Petersburg* (Fla.) *Times.* Used with permission.

22-3. Fire

You are making routine calls to the fire department and you receive this report from the dispatcher. Attribute information to fire department officials. Write the story in inverted pyramid order or hourglass form. Use yesterday as your time frame.

Information comes from Neil Heesacker, a spokesman for the fire department in your community. Firefighters responded to a fire at an apartment in a 32-unit apartment complex, Anderson Villa apartments, at 15758 S.E. Division St. at 6:39 a.m. The fire was brought under control at 7:05 a.m. The blaze caused an estimated $50,000 to the apartment building and $10,000 damage to the contents of the apartment. The value of the apartment building is estimated at $480,000. The family's belongings in the apartment that burned were valued at $80,000. The apartment was rented by Linda Lee Fuson. Her two sons, Kenneth A. J. Fuson, 10, and Michael Fuson, 14, were in the apartment at the time of the fire. Linda Fuson was not. She arrived some time after 6:40 a.m. Her whereabouts before then are unknown. The fire burned through the floor and blistered the gypsum walls and melted the family's television set. Three pet birds died. The fire also caused smoke damage to the apartment of Pat and Lisa Hampton, who live across the stairs from the Fuson family. The cause of the fire is under investigation. A neighbor, Darren Nitz, 31, is credited with saving Michael Fuson's life. He lives on the first floor, just below the Fusons' apartment. Michael Fuson suffered burns over a third of his body. He is in critical condition at Emanuel Hospital and Health Center's burn unit. He has second- and third-degree burns on his hands, arms, face, neck, back, buttocks and thighs. Kenneth Fuson was trapped in his bedroom. He died in the fire. Fire in an enclosed area such as an apartment can push temperatures to 1,700 degrees Fahrenheit near the ceiling and 1,000 degrees on the floor.

Information from interview with Darren Nitz: "About 6:35 a.m. I heard neighbors pounding on my door and yelling about the fire. I didn't think much about it at first, until someone said two children were trapped in the apartment. Michael was about seven feet from his bedroom door. He was saying 'I can't, I can't,' and rolling over and over. I said, 'We've got to get out of here.' I tried to grab hold of his arm but couldn't because he was so badly burned. I put him over my shoulder and carried him outside. He told me that Kenneth was still upstairs. I went back to the top of the stairs but the flames reached the front door. Another neighbor, Brad Lindsey, grabbed a fire extinguisher and followed me."

From Brad Lindsey, 24. "It was fully going when we got up there. Just after we got up them, it just vacuumed and shot right across the stairway. Nitz and I went back down the stairs. There was no way either of us could do anything about it."

22-4. Court terms quiz

Circle the correct answer:

1. At an arraignment a person is
    a. sentenced.
    b. formally charged with the crime and given a chance to enter a plea.
    c. given a chance to choose an attorney.
2. Change of venue is
    a. a change in the plea.
    b. a change in the location of the trial.
    c. a change in the charge.
3. A deposition is
    a. a decision to discontinue the case.
    b. deposing the judge in the case.
    c. a written statement of testimony.
4. A grand jury is
    a. a larger jury than is usually called.
    b. a group of citizens empowered by the court to investigate a possible crime.
    c. a jury that hears civil cases.
5. An injunction is
    a. an order by the court to cease an action.
    b. a point in the case when two motions are joined.
    c. a judgment by the court to discontinue the case.
6. A plaintiff is
    a. a person who is charged with the crime.
    b. a person who files a civil lawsuit.
    c. a person who is being sued in a civil lawsuit.
7. Nolo contendere means
    a. not guilty.
    b. guilty as charged.
    c. not fighting the charge.
8. A tort is
    a. a criminal case involving political charges.
    b. a civil case involving allegations of wrongdoing.
    c. a case involving a grand jury.
9. A true bill is
    a. a truthful finding by a judge.
    b. a finding of truth by a jury, resulting in a not-guilty verdict.
    c. an indictment issued by a grand jury.

10. A brief is

a. an abbreviated summary of the case.

    b. a legal document filed with the court by the lawyer.

    c. a brief summary the lawyer makes to the jury.

11. A docket is

    a. the room containing all the court files.

    b. a list of cases pending court action.

    c. a list of verdicts issued by the judge for the week.

12. A suspended sentence is:

    a. an order to delay the sentencing until further information is available.

    b. an order to cancel punishment if the defendant meets certain conditions.

    c. an order to drop all charges.

13. A plea bargain is

    a. an agreement between the prosecutor and defense attorney to accept a lesser charge and lesser sentence in exchange for a guilty or no-contest plea.

    b. an agreement between the plaintiff and defendant to bargain on the charges.

    c. an agreement between the plaintiff and the defendant to bargain for a settlement of a suit.

14. Extradition is

    a. a decision by the prosecutor to submit additional charges to the court.

    b. a procedure to move a person accused of a crime to a state where he or she currently is to the state where the crime occurred.

    c. a procedure to authorize extra police personnel to hunt for a criminal.

15. An affidavit is

    a. a written list of charges.

    b. a confession.

    c. a sworn statement of facts.

22-5. Mummy saga

This exercise, which will give you practice writing a continuing police/court case, is based on a real story, but the names have been changed. Write each part based on the information you have. Do not read ahead because you may not use anything in future exercises. However, when you write the next day's episode, you should always recap the basics of what happened. If your instructor prefers, you may change the locations to your own county.

People and place involved

Location: rural Knoxville, about 10 miles east of Galesburg in Knox County, Ill.

Knox County Sheriff Mark Shoemaker (source of most information)

Carol Truelove, 48, wife of the deceased. She is a registered nurse.

Carl Truelove, last seen alive in May, eight years ago, at age 40. His body was found in mummified condition.

Richard G. Cuspid, 56, a former Chicago-area dentist. He was a houseguest of Mrs. Truelove for the past year.

Curt Cousins, 44, of Cudahy, Wisconsin. He is Carol Truelove's cousin. He helped authorities gain entrance to her home.

Roger Cutter, Knox County coroner

Craig Truelove, 14, son of Carol Truelove

Cindy Truelove, 17, daughter of Carol Truelove

Roger Truelove, a Chicago attorney and brother of the late Carl Truelove. He fought to keep authorities from the house. He died five years ago of cancer.

Judge Ronald Tenold, presiding judge in Knox County District Court

1. Day One

Write a brief story based on this information, all of which comes from Mark Shoemaker. You are writing on deadline for an afternoon paper and cannot check much out, so this is a brief report. Use today as your time frame.

Shoemaker conducts a press conference at noon and says that sheriff's deputies have arrested Carol Truelove on a charge of failing to report a death. It is a Class A misdemeanor, punishable by a fine up to $1,000 and up to 364 days in jail. Shoemaker says his deputies entered Truelove's house at 11:30 a.m. today and found a corpse in a mummified state. The corpse, believed to be Carl Truelove, was wrapped in blankets and was lying on a bed in a back room of the house. Carl Truelove had not been seen for eight years. Carol Truelove had told people he was very ill, and she would not let anyone see him.

Police had no probable cause to search the house previously. They entered today, despite her objections, because a relative had let them in the house and told them about the corpse. Shoemaker will not release the relative's name. Shoemaker says of the corpse: "His skin was dried up like shoe leather, and he just shriveled up. We believe he was kept a long time in a basement lounge chair. Although it was obvious he had been dead for eight years, the family sincerely thought he was fine, the way he was being treated. They changed his clothes and bedding just like he was sick. There's also evidence that they moved him around the house to different rooms and chairs. There was no strong odor in the home and something had to be done at the time of death to preserve the body."

He said the body had on pajama bottoms, underwear and socks. "Everything was very neat, very clean." He would not speculate what was done. An autopsy is expected at the end of this week. Foul play is not suspected, but the incident is under investigation. Mrs. Truelove's houseguest, Richard G. Cuspid, also was arrested on the same misdemeanor charge. They will be arraigned tomorrow morning. You have many questions, but Shoemaker says he will not comment further until the couple has been officially charged and arraigned. Both suspects were booked and held in the county jail.

2. Day Two

The arraignment. Use today as your time frame. The news is very brief, but don't forget to include your background.

Judge Ronald Tenold presided in Knox County Circuit Court at 9 a.m. today. Carol Truelove and Richard Cuspid both pleaded guilty to the misdemeanor charge of failing to report a death. The judge did not sentence them at this time. He ordered a pre-sentence investigation. The two were released on their own recognizance. Carol Truelove did not speak other than to plead guilty. Cuspid complained that he had not been allowed to post his $100 bail because the sheriff's office would not accept silver coins as payment. He also complained of conditions at the jail and said he had not had anything to eat or drink because "I only eat pure food" and his requests for distilled water, tuna and halibut had been denied. Write your story on deadline. Sheriff Shoemaker tells you after the arraignment that the charge was the only one he could make because "eight years is not exactly timely reporting of a death." The coroner is still checking cause of death. State law requires people to notify the coroner of a death within 24 hours.

3. Day Two - next step

You have just written your deadline story when you get a call from Sheriff Mark Shoemaker's office. He is going to have a press conference in 30 minutes. At the press conference, he gives you this information; rewrite your story.

We have rearrested Carol Truelove and Richard Cuspid on additional charges. They were arrested within minutes of their release as they were leaving the courthouse and were taken back to jail pending another arraignment later today on the new charges. Mrs. Truelove has been charged with one count of forgery for allegedly signing her husband's name to fabricate a power of attorney eight years ago. Cuspid was charged with one count of conspiracy to commit forgery for signing his name to the document as a witness. Both are forgery charges, punishable by up to three years in prison. The document gave Carol the right to control money in Carl's bank account. You have many questions about the case and the sheriff gives you this information in response:

"Apparently Carol Truelove and members of her family believed the corpse of Carl Truelove was still alive. They felt he could talk with them and everyone in the family admits to communicating with them. It's just very bizarre. We are currently investigating religious aspects of this."

He says Carol Truelove wants her husband's body returned to her home, but the sheriff's office is checking on health codes to see if this can be prevented legally. He says he and his deputies had checked on Carl Truelove over the years but had never been able to gain admittance to the house. He says Carl, a bookkeeper for Drainclean Plumbing, failed to report to work and the owner had notified the sheriff's office. But he says he had no probable cause to get a search warrant, so he just took Carol's word for it that her husband was very ill and could not have visitors. He says Cuspid had been her houseguest for a year and is believed to be part of a religious group or cult that believes in some sort of healing involving dentistry and herbs and special diet. He says Cuspid was introduced by Carol Truelove's late brother-in-law, Roger Truelove, who drew up the power-of-attorney document. Carl Truelove was a diabetic. The coroner is still checking cause of death. He says he gained access to the house when Carol Truelove's cousin, Curt Cousins, had visited the house and then notified the sheriff's office of the corpse. Cousins let the sheriff's deputies in the house. The children, who are honor students in school, have been temporarily placed in foster care. He stills says no foul play is suspected in connection with the corpse. Write your story for a later edition of today's paper.

4. Day Three

Carol Truelove and Richard Cuspid were arraigned yesterday on the new charges before Judge Ronald Tenold. Both pleaded not guilty. Tenold set bail at $20,000 for each, but neither could post it, so they remain in the county jail. In related developments, the coroner, Roger Cutter, ruled that Carl Truelove, a lifelong diabetic, died about eight years ago from insulin shock (caused by a lack of insulin). Cutter said the mummified body was dehydrated but had been preserved by some herbal mixture. The children remain in protective custody. The sheriff said the state is still trying to get an order to bury the remains of the corpse.

Epilogue: Not for your story. The woman was convicted of forgery and received two years probation and her houseguest was also convicted and sentenced to 30 months on probation. The corpse was finally buried by a state order, because officials feared the wife would take it back into her home and continue tending to it.

22-6. Campus crime statistics

Access Security on Campus, a Web site of college and university crime statistics and write a story comparing crime rates for your school (if they are available) with those of other schools near you or of your choice. Check out other links as well. Interview a law enforcement officer in your university about problems on campus. If your community or campus police department has a Web site, check it against the national site. You can access Security on Campus through the Web site for this book or directly at *http://www.campussafety.org*.

Check the Web site devoted to crime stories as well to see how crime stories can be written and how many interesting stories are available at this all-crime site if it is still online: APBOnline *http://www.apbonline.com*.

22-7. Court cases

Write a story based on a court opinion for a case in your state (or other if you prefer). Access Findlaw from the Web site for this book or directly at: *<www.findlaw.com>*.

Click into Cases and Codes and then click on State Cases and Codes until you find your state. Check any of the court cases; the Court of Appeals cases are often interesting. Find a case and write a news story based on the court document. For example, here is an Alaska case about a man who attacked his ex-wife because he couldn't find his wallet. It is rich in detail. *http://www.touchngo.com/ap/html/ap-1607.htm*

22-8. Style test

Correct the style errors and poor or inappropriate wording:

1. John Powers, a spokesman for the Pasco Sheriff's department, said the boys left a 50 pound box of milky ways on a bench.

2. The robber was described as a black man in his middle 20's about five ft., 10 in. and 140 lbs.

3. The fire in the apartment at the 2,700 block of Northeast 30th Pl. caused an estimated 9000 dollars worth of damage.

4. The boy suffered second and third degree burns over 1/3 of his body.

5. The weapon was a 22-caliber handgun.

6. Firemen arrived on the scene about six thirty in the morning.

7. Fire in an apartment can reach 1,700 ^{0} near the ceiling.

8. The defendent was sentenced to five years' in prison.

9. The mummified body was found on January 30.

10. The plaintiff prays for judgement in excess of ten thousand dollars.

Disasters, Weather and Tragedy

23

This chapter will give you practice writing a follow-up story to the textbook plane crash, another type of disaster story, a weather feature and a chance to familiarize yourself with online resources. Check the Web site for this book at *http://info.wadsworth.com/rich*.

23-1. Plane crash – Day 2 story

This is the second-day story to follow the plane crash exercise in your textbook. This is a deadline assignment. You have about an hour. Use whatever human-interest material you need for the mainbar. You do not have to use all of this material.

Many of the facts have changed, including the number of dead and injured. You have received a passenger list so you now have the names of those who died and those who survived, but the list will be published separately so don't worry about including it in your story. You are contacting relatives for some of your information – there will be separate sidebars on them – and officials of the airline, the airport, the National Transportation Safety Board, hospitals, and so on. Not all the dead have been identified. You have contacted some relatives, and you will be at the airport to meet others who are arriving on two flights. Delta Airlines has flown in the relatives free of charge. One plane, Flight 222, is coming from Dallas; another, Flight 333, is arriving at 10 a.m. from New York.

Rescue workers worked throughout the night to clear the last of the bodies from the plane and the area. The wreckage of the plane is still on the edge of the runway. Investigators from the NTSB are still combing the wreckage. Although this concourse remains closed, the airport is open and planes are taking off on schedule at other concourses.

Delta Airlines spokesman I.M. Devastated says the death toll was higher than originally expected. The total death toll at this point is 234, with 50 survivors. Devastated says it is possible that some infants who were not on the passenger list might also have died, raising the death toll, but he is not certain at this time.

Included in the death toll are the pilot and two co-pilots and five of the six flight attendants. Also, five people who originally survived have died overnight in area hospitals. All but five of the remaining survivors are in the hospital. The five others were released last night.

Most of the injured have broken bones and 15 of them have severe burns. The burn victims are at the University of Kansas Medical Center. The others are at Liberty Hospital and St. Luke's Hospital.

The following information comes from other reporters but you may use it in your mainbar:

From Elsa M. Nurse, spokeswoman for KU Medical Center: She said she has never seen such extensive burns in all her 33 years at the hospital. "It's a wonder they survived at all," she said. "All the burn victims are in shock."

From St. Luke's Hospital: Every doctor and nurse has worked double shifts. The emergency room is filled with at least 40 area residents who are donating blood. "It's the least I can do," said Steve Marcus, 19, a University of Kansas sophomore. "We were lucky. My brother, Bob, was on that plane and he survived. He's here with a broken leg, a broken collar bone and a concussion, but at least he's alive." Marcus and his brother live at 2330 New Hampshire St. in Lawrence. Bob is 21, a senior majoring in journalism at KU. Bob Marcus is one of three survivors from Lawrence. Forty-five of the people who died also were from Lawrence.

From survivor Annie Grace Lucky, 47, a Dallas resident: She had flown to Missouri to visit a friend in Kansas City. She was one of the five released from the hospital. She was at the airport arranging with authorities to provide her limousine transportation to Dallas. This was her first plane trip. "I had always had a fear of flying," Lucky said. "I figured at my age, it was time to get over it. Now I'm afraid I won't. I'll never fly again. I expect this airline to get me home on the ground."

From survivor John Microchip, computer salesman: He works for Bigstate Computers in Dallas, corporate headquarters for his firm. He came to Kansas City for a business conference. He is in St. Luke's with a broken leg, a broken neck, several ruptured vertebrae and a broken arm. He said he saw the thunderclouds around the jet as it circled the airport, but he wasn't concerned at first. When the passengers behind him cried out in alarm at the turbulence, he said he told them, "Don't worry about it. It's just a typical thunderstorm. We're going to be safe." Then he added: "Suddenly it felt as though somebody stepped on us. The plane kind of rocked, and people began screaming and yelling. Nobody was expecting it. I saw the ground coming up. Then we hit. The plane bounced once. Then it bounced again. I opened my eyes, and there I was dangling 30 feet above the grass, still strapped into my seat belt. I thought that I had either arrived in heaven or on earth. Then I unbuckled my seat belt and fell to the ground."

From Janet Sorrow of Dallas: She lost her whole family. She arrived from Dallas on the morning flight. She was sobbing as she was escorted by airline personnel to the Delta Airlines hospitality suite where officials were waiting for her. Airline officials tried to stop reporters from talking to her, but she said before she went in that her husband, Bob, and her three children – Janet, 2, Robert Jr., 3, and Amy, 6 – were coming to Kansas City to start a new life. Bob was a carpenter and there wasn't any work in Dallas because of the oil recession, so he finally got a job in Kansas City after nine months of unemployment in Texas. "We were so happy at getting a new chance. I stayed behind and planned to join them in a few weeks because I had to handle the final details of selling our house. Now I have no home, no husband, no family. I wish I had died with them."

From Jennifer Agony of Dallas: She is 25, wife of crash victim, James L. Agony. She said her husband was taking a long weekend to visit friends in Kansas City. "Two months ago he got bumped from another Delta Airlines flight and was given a free ticket for another round trip. They told him he could fly anywhere, anytime he wanted to. He made the wrong choice," she said, sobbing.

From NTSB investigators: They said they are not sure yet, but they blame the crash on weather conditions. The winds were between 60 and 65 mph at the time the plane crashed, and lightning was in the area. Retired Coast Guard Adm. Patrick Bursely, the lead NTSB investigator, said it appears the plane might have hit a microburst. That is an upward air current surrounding a center of downward winds. It's known as wind shear and it will force a plane to plummet, he explains. It's a dangerous weather phenomenon.

Bursley seemed very upset. He said there is a question whether the pilot had received the most up-to-date weather forecast before he attempted his landing. Bursley said the black box has been recovered. He said: "There is indication of a weather forecast being delivered to controllers some 10 minutes before the accident, and that was not passed along to the pilot. It appears that both controllers involved and the pilots involved in this accident were not concerned about the immediate weather conditions."

He said controllers were advised about 15 minutes before the crash that cumulonimbus clouds had formed east of the airport. Such clouds are often associated with thunderstorms, which could contain violent wind shears. The latest weather forecast the pilot received before the crash was an hour old, he said. He added that he is basing all that information from the recording in the black box, which was recovered last night.

The National Weather Service reported that at the time the plane was making its final approach, a huge thunderstorm was 5,000 feet above the airport and was unleashing winds and lightning. The storm only arose over the airport area about 30 minutes before the plane crashed. Bursely said the pilot never got that information. The plane was in a landing pattern at 2,000 to 3,000 feet at that time.

From Kansas City Medical Examiner, Dr. Richard C. Froede: He is in charge of death certificates for all the victims. He said that determining the identity of all the dead could take days. He said so far, about 215 of the dead have been identified, but he is waiting for dental records to confirm the identification of the others.

"There are fragments of bodies that have been recovered. This was a gruesome crash. We may get to the point where some bodies may never be identified. I'm amazed anyone survived."

23-2. Explosion mainbar

This is the kind of explosion that can happen in any community. Write a main story. You also should evaluate whether some of the material should not be used for ethical reasons.

You are a reporter for *The Sun,* a daily newspaper in San Bernardino, Calif. It is shortly after 8 a.m. You are listening to the police radio and you hear a report that there has been an explosion. You call the police dispatcher and learn that a gasoline pipeline exploded in the same neighborhood in which a 69-car runaway freight train derailed about two weeks ago, either an ironic or relevant coincidence. When the freight train derailed, it crashed into a string of homes and killed two crew members in the train and two boys in one home. Police spokesman Gary Fahnestrock tells you: "There has been an explosion. We haven't sorted anything out yet." Your editor tells you to get to the scene. You get to the scene where confusion reigns. You gather as much information as you can and return to the newspaper to write this story on deadline. You have about 45 minutes until deadline. You have gathered the information that follows for a location map. Here are your notes for the story:

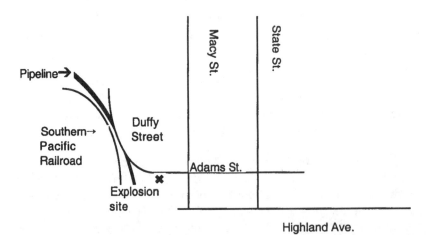

The explosion occurred at 8:11 a.m. in the neighborhood bounded by Duffy Street and Highland Ave., exactly the same area where the freight train derailed two weeks ago. When you arrive at Duffy Street, you see flames shooting about 100 feet into the air and seven homes on fire. You try to talk to as many people as possible. Here are your sources:

David Andries, an official of the Calnev gas company: He says the explosion was caused by a 14-inch gasoline pipeline that ruptured. The pipeline, which is buried six feet underground, carries unleaded fuel from Colton (a neighboring community) to Nevada. He says it sprayed fuel on the houses when it ruptured. "We don't know the cause of the break. It could have been the train, obviously," he says.

Gregory Garcia, a spokesman for the mayor of San Bernardino: About 700 people have been evacuated to the Red Cross evacuation center. The center has been set up at the Job Corps Center, 3753 Kerry St.

Theresa Schorder, a Red Cross worker: By 10 a.m. 30 residents from Duffy and Donald streets neighborhoods arrived at the center. Two vans and a bus are being used for the evacuation.

Paul Allaire, San Bernardino Fire Department spokesman: Two people have died in a home on Duffy Street. One body was burned beyond recognition. The other victim is believed to be a man. Firefighters are looking for a third victim in the home.

San Bernardino Councilwoman Valerie Pope-Ludlam who was at the scene: "A woman ran out of her house, she left behind her sister and her cousin and a 6-month-old baby inside, and she looked back and the house blew up behind her."

Phil Arviso, a council aide: He said he talked to the woman whom Pope-Ludlam mentioned. He said she was Robbie Brown of 2327 Duffy St. He said Brown said her relatives, Keesha Jefferson, Charlene Jefferson and Charlene's baby were in the house. "She actually said her house blew up behind her as she came out. The house is gone. If anybody was in there, they went with it."

Bill Stewart, an insurance agent who was visiting a client, Martha Franklin in a house in the 2300 block of Donald Street which borders Adams Street (about a block away from the explosion): "We were sitting at the table and we heard this loud noise, and it just started getting bigger. I ran to the window and looked out and could see nothing but smoke; then we both hit the floor. We waited for it to blow over, but it didn't go away. Then we started to head for the door and when she opened the door, the smoke just started rolling in. We looked outside. The grass was burning – green grass burning. Everything was burning, even the concrete."

Calnev pipeline General Manager Jed Robinson: He said the pipeline can carry more than 3.3 million gallons of fuel jet fuel, gasoline and diesel – which flows through the 14-inch pipeline daily. The pipeline was carrying unleaded gasoline. He said valves along the pipe fall into place whenever anything in the pipe starts to flow backward, toward Colton where the pipeline starts. He said a valve near the fire may not be completely closed, and that could influence the time it takes to put out the fire. "With that kind of a volatile fuel, you have to use some sort of foam. Normally where there is not an awful lot of fuel, you just contain it and try and let it burn out." He said he didn't know how much fuel is in the pipe.

Miretta Brumlow, a resident of 2351 Adams St. near the site: She was at the first aid center set up at Macy Street. She was still wearing a nightgown. "I felt my whole house shake. I thought it was an earthquake. Then I looked out and I saw the fire and I just started crying. I ran to the bedroom and got my daughter and grandson out, then I started looking for my pets, and then I just had to get out. I think my cats are still in there. Everything I own was in that house." She said she is a student at San Bernardino Valley College, but she hasn't attended school since the railroad disaster because she's been afraid to leave her children at home. "Thank God I didn't go to my class at eight o'clock this morning."

San Bernardino City Attorney Jim Penman, who toured the area this morning from a helicopter: "We were assured by the pipeline people it was safe (after the railroad accident) and the experts who examined it said there was no danger."

From hospital officials: Seven burn victims were admitted to the San Bernardino County Medical Center. Their conditions were not available. Other people admitted and treated were: Tina Blackburn – in serious condition with second- and third-degree burns over 15 percent of her body; Michael Howard with burns on his hands; his wife, Janet Howard, with third-degree burns and their two children, Shirley, 1, and LaKedra,2, who were being treated for smoke inhalation. Diane Tucker was treated for minor cuts.

Observations and general information you receive from various sources: Southern California Gas Co. workers were in the neighborhood to shut off gas lines to avoid any possibility of natural gas explosion, they said. A thick cloud of gray-black smoke from the explosion was reported visible as far away as Riverside and Ontario (neighboring communities). Highland Avenue at Macy was closed to motorists.

You are out of time. You must return to the newspaper and write the story. Use today as your time frame. This story will be in print in about 90 minutes.

Based on a story from *The* (San Bernardino, Calif.,) *Sun,* Used with permission.

23-3. Explosion sidebar

You have written your mainbar on deadline, and you are now reporting a human-interest story for a sidebar for the next day's newspaper. You go to the Red Cross shelter set up at the Job Corps Center on Kerry Street to interview residents who are there because they have been evacuated from their homes. The general reaction you get is that the residents are very angry. The freight train derailment two weeks ago traumatized them, and they thought their homes were safe after that disaster. Here are your sources:

Georgia Mitchell of 2337 Duffy St.: Her house was destroyed and her daughter, a son-in-law and two grandchildren were injured. Two weeks ago she watched the train derail in front of her home. "If it wasn't safe for us to live, why'd they tell us it's OK to move back there?"

Maxie Charles of 2441 San Benito Court: He said the federal government should step provide emergency relief. "This should be declared a disaster area. If they want to keep these pipelines, they should pay us off and we will be happy to move out."

Bonita Campbell, of San Carlo Avenue: She was walking around the Job Corps ground in the gown, robe and slippers she wore when the explosion occurred. Her family got out of their home safely; her two dogs were waiting in her car. "Right now I don't know what to think. I don't know what to do. I know I can't continue to live like this not knowing what's going to happen."

Vincent Hemphill, 25, who grew up in the house at 2604 Duffy St.: He said even if his home survived, he won't go back. No one should return to those unlucky streets, he said. "They had no damn business trying to patch no pipe up anyway. They should have discontinued that until they fixed it. (Referring to the neighborhood): It's messed up. I think they should just, like, take the whole neighborhood and move us out of there. It's a disaster for all of us now. "

Patrick Thomas of 2313 Adams St.: He was holding his daughter, Lisa, 15 months old. His home that he rents was unscathed by the train wreck. But yesterday when he last saw his home, flames were crawling up one side. The home was situated five houses away from another house that blew up on Adams Street. "I am mad. I am mad as hell – at the railroad, at whoever put that fuel line in, at whoever built those houses over a fuel line, at the city for not doing something."

Mark Kingston, area resident: "It makes me sick that this fire happened, especially if somebody knew it needed to be repaired. Somebody ought to be hung out to dry."

Clemmie Williams, 51, of San Benito Court: He says the right side of his face still stings where a medic smeared white salve over a burn. He said two days ago he whiffed something in the air near his home that smelled like a mixture of fuel and ammonia. The odor lasted about 10 minutes, so he let it pass without concern. "They (Calnev officials) said there was no leakage so we assumed it was OK."

Based on a story from *The* (San Bernardino, Calif.,) *Sun,* Used with permission.

23-4. Coping Sidebar

Choose a type of disaster that your community might experience: floods, tornadoes, hurricanes or earthquakes. Using the online resources linked to the Web site for this book, research the topic and write a sidebar about tips for coping. If you have disaster relief officials or Red Cross officials in your community, you could interview them for additional information. Does your community have a disaster emergency plan? Some of you might write a story about that. Check the links to disaster resources on the Web site for this chapter in the textbook.

23-5. Basic weather feature

Write a feature story about the weather. First brainstorm several angles you might take if you are having a hot, cold, dry, wet or other unusual stretch of weather. Interview students and other people on campus about how they are reacting to the weather. Is business in your area affected by the weather? Interview some business people, city or campus officials about costs they might be incurring because of the weather. Make sure you get human interest angles. See the examples in your textbook.

Check the forecast for your area and record high and low temperatures for the month or day by accessing any of the weather sites on the Web site for this chapter or linking directly to *<www.weather.com>*.

23-6. Covering grief

Check the grief resources on the Internet by accessing the Web site for this book. Click into Griefnet or Yahoo's bereavement resources. Read some of the personal essays and sites from people who have experienced tragedy. If you had to interview them, what questions would you ask? Make a list of questions or concerns you might have and discuss them with the class. If your instructor prefers, write a feature story based on the information on these sites or interview classmates and/or other people about a loss they might have experienced of a relative, friend or pet. For a possible sidebar on how to cope with grief, check some of these coping sites, linked to the Web site for this book or listed here. *http://griefnet.org/*
http://uk.dir.yahoo.com/health/Mental_Health/Bereavement/index.html.

Profiles

24

The best way to learn how to write profiles is to interview someone. But for purposes of practice, these exercises will help you learn the important elements of writing profiles. You'll find links to online resources for these exercises on the Web site for this book:

http://info.wadsworth.com/rich9808.

24-1. Autobiographical profile

If you are applying for a job or for graduate school, you are often asked to write an autobiographical essay. Writing about yourself is one of the hardest types of profiles. To do this well, you should interview your friends, teachers and family. For exercise purposes, however, you may just interview yourself. Here are some questions you should ask yourself. If you were interviewing someone else, you should also ask these questions.

First write a facts box and fill in the answers about yourself.

Part I. Facts box

Favorite books:

Favorite movies:

Favorite song:

Best advice I ever received:

Heroes or heroines:

I chose my current field of study or career because:

One of the hardest decisions I had to make was:

If I could be anything I wanted, I'd be:

My favorite childhood memory is:

I would describe myself as (list character traits):

My friends would describe me as:

When I graduate, I'd like to (go, do, be):

If I could change something about myself, it would be:

The main obstacles I have faced or am facing are:

Add any other questions you think might be helpful.

Part II. Free writing

For the next 10 to 15 minutes just write your thoughts, feelings, an experience or anything that comes to your mind. Do not stop and think. Write in stream of consciousness without any concern about grammar, spelling, or content. No one is going to see this but you.

Part III. Description

Write a description of your room, emphasizing items that are meaningful to you. Describe pictures on your wall, specific books, magazines, stuffed animals or anything that characterizes your environment. Imagine that you are interviewing someone else and you are observing his or her environment. Just jot down items if you prefer.

Part IV. Analysis

Looking at the information you have compiled, analyze it for any patterns or any specific details that reflect your personality. Imagine that these are notes you have taken from an interview with a source.

Here are some questions to ask yourself as you analyze your notes:

• What have I learned or observed about myself that surprises me?

• What one dominant impression do I give, based on the information I have compiled?

• What impression would I like people to have of me?

• Are there any patterns I observe in this information?

• Was there a turning point in my life that made me decide to go to this college or choose my current career field?

• What details about me stand out most?

Part V. Write a profile

Using the third-person voice, write a profile about yourself as though you were a stranger you described in the first four parts of this exercise. You may add quotes as necessary. Try to show yourself in action by describing some of your idiosyncrasies, habits and the things you do often. Set the scene for your profile and put yourself in it. Add background information as necessary to help the reader understand you and how you got to this point in your life. Although the newsworthy angle and focus are strained, you could imagine that this will be part of a series of profiles or vignettes for a yearbook or a newspaper article about faces on campus.

24-2. Web autobiography

Writing a resume for the Web differs from print. Using some of the information you have written in the previous exercise (or starting from scratch), write an autobiography in less than five paragraphs or less than 22 lines (include a line for each space between paragraphs). What can you say that would tease a reader to know more about you? See if you can describe yourself in one screen for a Web resume, which will give you a head start for planning an online resume in Chapter 26.

24-3. Background research for profile

Choose a famous person or campus athlete you would like to interview. Do background research by checking magazines, newspaper articles, library resources or databases. Write a list of questions you would ask. You can link to online databases for celebrities from the Web site for this chapter.

24-4. Slice-of-life profile

You are interviewing a mail carrier for a slice-of-life profile about people who work in your community. This person isn't very quotable and she doesn't consider her job extraordinary. But you have to find something interesting for your lead. Consider an anecdotal lead or a show-in-action lead. Using these notes, which are not in good order, write a brief profile:

The letter carrier is Nancy Workman. She has worked for the U.S. Postal Service for five and a half years. Her walking route covers approximately 23 square miles. She spends between four and four and a half hours each day delivering the mail. "I come in each morning at 7:15 a.m., and I sort the mail for about three hours. Then I deliver the mail, and after that, I work at the office, preparing for the next day until 3:15 p.m. Letter carriers choose their own delivery routes based on seniority. I love meeting the people on my route and getting to know them. I chose my route because it was a flat walking route. Most letter carriers prefer driving routes, but driving just never appealed to me. Walking is tremendous medicine, as it's a great time for reflection."

She said winter was the most difficult time to deliver the mail, not only because of the weather, but because she encounters fewer people to talk to. Workman estimates that she walks almost 12 miles each day. Consequently, she closely monitors weather forecasts. "Once you're out there, you have no shelter. There's no place you can hide. The worst thing is sitting at home, worrying the night before a major storm. I have problems sleeping on those nights, just thinking about the coming storm. I love the outdoors, and I love the freedom of the street." Encounters with dogs are a minor job hazard. She carries dog mace in her dusty blue mailbag. "I've only had a dog bite me once, and it was very minor, more like a mosquito bite," Workman said. "Dog poop, though, can really ruin your day."

Workman said she enjoys the unpredictability she faces in the weather and in other aspects of her job. "Each day I come in, and I have no idea how much mail there will be," Workman said. "Some days catalogs are the enemy. Lately, Victoria's Secret has been just crazy — sending out new catalogs all the time." Workman plans to remain a letter carrier indefinitely. "I really do love this job," she said. "I plan to keep delivering the mail until I can't walk anymore." The most unusual experience she had was when one of her patrons failed to pick up his mail for several days. "His mail just kept piling up, and after a while, it worried me. I didn't want to overreact. But then I noticed the front door of his house. His screen door was covered with flies. I went next door and asked the man's neighbors to call the police. The police discovered that the middle-aged man had died of a heart attack several days ago. I was hoping I was wrong, but I had a really eerie feeling about the whole situation. It was really scary because I knew this man, and suddenly he was dead."

24-5. Rosa Parks, Charles Kuralt or other famous people

The Academy of Achievement Web site contains very brief profiles and great question-answer interviews with many of the world's great achievers, including Rosa Parks and Charles Kuralt. You might also choose interviews with athletes such as Julius Erving or Duke University basketball coach Mike Krzyzewski. Access the Web site from the chapter for this book or directly from *<www.achievement.org>*. Then go to gallery of achievers frames version, so you'll have to click on a category of interest (public service) to locate Rosa Parks and Charles Kuralt. Read the question/answer interviews and write a profile. If you have audio software on your computer, you can listen to the interview. You also could check other Web sites for additional information.

Computer-assisted Journalism

25

This chapter will give you experience using spreadsheets to analyze databases. These exercises will focus on simple database calculations in a spreadsheet such as Excel. A first step in computer-assisted journalism is using a spreadsheet to calculate statistics for your stories. You can link to resources on the Web site for this book:
http://info.wadsworth.com/authors/rich.

25-1. Sort and calculate #1

What media occupations expected to experience growth by 2010? Which pay the most? Here are projections of the U.S. Bureau of Labor Statistics. Copy this data in Excel or other spreadsheet program. Then follow directions to sort and calculate the number of job changes and the percent and the most lucrative. Numbers here are listed in thousands of jobs. **Be sure to save your original worksheet and each calculation in a different worksheet so you don't lose your data.** To widen the first column, place your cursor on the bar between A and B and stretch it when it changes from a fat to a thin cross.

- **Sort #1:** Sort first by which jobs pay the highest median earnings. Highlight all the columns (so the order stays in tact) and then sort by the earnings column (F). Put your fat cursor on Row 19 (or whichever is your last row) in Column F (don't include the labels in the top Row 7) and move upward through all rows and across to the left. (If you start on the first row of numbers in the left column, move all to the right). Then pull down the Sort descending button. The point is to sort by Column F in descending order to see who makes the most money. (You should get art directors at the top.)
- **Calculate number change:** Subtract the number of total employment in 2000 from the number in 2010.
- **Sort #2:** Now sort by the occupations with the greatest change in numbers of employees.
- **Calculate percentage change:** Figure the percentage by dividing the change figure by the original figure – (=d10/b10).
- **Sort #3:** Then sort by the greatest percentage change.

Here is the working document:

	A	B	C	D	E	F
1		**Total**		**2000-2010**		**Median annual**
2		**employment**		**change**		**earnings**
3		**(000's)**		**in total**		**(Dollars)**
4				**employment**		
5				**Number**		
6	**Occupation**	**2000**	**2010**	**(000's)**	**Percent**	
10	Graphic designers	190	241			34,570
11	Public relations specialists	137	186			39,580
12	Photographers	131	153			22,300
13	Writers and authors	126	162			42,270
14	Editors	122	149			39,370
15	Public relations managers	74	101			54,540
16	Announcers	71	68			19,800
17	Art directors	47	56			56,880
18	Broadcast technicians	36	40			26,950
19	Film and video editors	16	20			34,160

Source: U.S. Bureau of Labor Statistics

25-2. Sort and calculate #2

You are writing a story about sexually transmitted diseases. The U.S. Centers for Disease Control releases annual reports on sexually transmitted diseases. A recent report says that chlamydia, a bacterial organism, is one of the fastest growing sexually transmitted diseases. You notice that the rates are much higher for women than men and you want to write about the highest incidence in age groups. Copy the following chart and then calculate totals.

- Add to get totals.
- Subtract to calculate the difference of rates between men and women.
- Calculate the percentage differences.
- Sort in descending order to find which age group has the greatest percentage difference.
- Sort in descending order to find which age group has the highest numbers.

Working statistics:

age group	male	female	difference	%difference
10-14	451	8,717		
15-19	19,298	139,256		
20-24	25,439	104,929		
25-29	12,625	38,553		
30-34	6,326	14,733		
35-39	3,280	6,441		
40-44	1,537	2,659		
45-54	1,124	1,536		
55-64	271	876		
65+	266	291		
totals				

To find out more if you want to write a story, access the Web site for the Centers for Disease Control. These statistics may differ from more current ones that may be available on the site.

Charts: To make a chart with the Excel chart wizard, highlight the figures you want to include, such as the age group with the highest number of chlamydia cases. Click the chart wizard and select the type of chart you want. Have fun.

25-3. Write a story from statistics

Write a news story from following press release and statistical chart about income by educational attainment. The press release is basic but boring. Analyze the statistics and supplement with more information from online or sources you interview. The statistics are rather dated but they were the most recent available in 2001 from the U.S. Census Bureau. For further information, access the Census Bureau online and look for the report, "What's it Worth? Field of Training and Economic Status
http://www.census.gov/population/www/socdemo/education/p70-72.html

Technical Degrees Worth More, U.S. Census Bureau Reports

College graduates who work full time and have a bachelor's degree in engineering earn the highest average monthly pay ($4,680), while those with education degrees earn the lowest ($2,802), according to a report based on 1996 data released today by the Commerce Department's Census Bureau.

These data on the earnings potential of different college majors should not be confused with the results of Census 2000, which are being released over the next three years.

"Majoring in a technical field does pay off even if you don't finish a four-year degree," said Kurt Bauman, co-author with Camille Ryan of What's It Worth? Field of Training and Economic Status, 1996. "The average person with a vocational certificate earns around $200 more per month than the average high school graduate; but if the certificate is in an engineering-related field, the boost in earnings is close to $800."

(You can analyze the top earnings and other highlights based on the statistics you should sort for highest salaries, difference between pay for men and women or people of color and other information you glean from the statistics.)

Monthly income by education, sex, race, ethnicity and age
(Statistics for highest level of education completed = age 18 and over)
B= base less than 100,000

	High school	Some college	Vocat-ional	Associate degree	Bachelor's degree	Master's degree	Profess-ional degree	Doctorate
TOTAL	$1,493	$1,755	$1,830	$2,216	$2,909	$3,763	$6,304	$5,214
Sex								
Men	$1,950	$2,225	$2,428	$2,739	$3,739	$4,621	$6,957	$5,847
Women	$1,086	$1,325	$1,430	$1,805	$2,098	$2,860	$4,620	$3,645
Race and ethnicity								
White	$1,549	$1,824	$1,863	$2,247	$2,976	$3,821	$6,464	$5,438
Non-Hispanic	$1,579	$1,861	$1,885	$2,233	$3,008	$3,822	$6,555	$5,515
Black	$1,191	$1,448	$1,546	$2,046	$2,567	$3,166	B	
Hispanic*	$1,212	$1,426	$1,556	$2,473	$2,226	$3,614	$4,955	B
Age								
18 to 29 years old	$1,070	$1,025	$1,411	$1,546	$1,943	$2,360	$2,473	B
30 to 49 years old	$1,716	$2,159	$2,024	$2,481	$3,310	$4,042	$6,690	$5,708
50 years old & over	$1,514	$2,054	$1,758	$2,081	$2,871	$3,645	$6,458	$4,842

25-4. Analyze data: Unmarried couples

The following information from the 2000 U.S. Census shows the numbers of unwed people living together. Analyze the data and write a news story (including interviews with your friends or unmarried people you know who are living together). Analyze the information for these questions:

- What part of the country has the highest number of unwed couples?
- What age group is the highest for unwed couples?
- For more information, access the U.S. Census for families and living arrangements:

http://www.census.gov/population/www/socdemo/hh-fam/p20-537_00.html

Numbers in the thousands	
UNMARRIED PARTNER HOUSEHOLDS	3,822
REGION	
Northeast	692
Midwest	888
South	1,195
West	1,047
METROPOLITAN STATUS	
Central City	1,388
Suburban	1,742
Nonmetropolitan	692
MARITAL STATUS OF HOUSEHOLDER	
Married Spouse Present	5
Married Spouse Absent	80
Widowed	153
Divorced	1,324
Separated	198
Never Married	2,062
SIZE OF HOUSEHOLD	
Two members	1,975
Three members	775
Four members	614
Five members	293
Six or more members	166
AGE OF HOUSEHOLDER	
Under 20 years	91
20-24 years	633
25-29 years	762
30-34 years	598
35-39 years	503
40-44 years	431
45-54 years	477
55-64 years	213
65+ years	112

Media Jobs and Internships

26

This chapter will provide information to supplement the textbook material on how to seek internships and jobs. Click into the Web site for this book for many online resources: *http://info.wadsworth.com/rich*.

26-1. Research the organization

Before you decide where to apply for a job or internship, you should conduct research about the kinds of opportunities that are available and about the organization to which you wish to apply. Most organizations now have sites on the World Wide Web, so be sure to check for them and research the organization before you apply.

You should also familiarize yourself with directories that list the company address, phone numbers and key officials. But never rely on directories to be up to date with names of people. Always call to find out to whom you should send your resume.

Using the directories that apply to your field, list at least three organizations in which you would be interested for an internship or a job. Here are a few directories, most of which give circulation, key managers, addresses and telephone numbers:

Newspaper Directories
- *Media Encyclopedia – Working Press of the Nation – Newspaper Directory.*
- *Editor & Publisher Yearbook.* Lists newspapers by daily and weekly publications.
- *Gale's Directory of Publications.* Lists magazines, journals and newspapers.

Broadcast Media Directories
- *Media Encyclopedia –Working Press of the Nation. Television and Radio Directory.*
- *Broadcasting Yearbook.*
- *Television/Cable Factbook.*

Magazines and Public Relations Directories

- *Gale's Directory of Publications.* Lists magazines, journals and newspapers.
- *Media Encyclopedia –Working Press of the Nation – Magazine Directory.*
- *Gebbie House Magazine Directory.* A guide to company internal magazines.
- *Bowkers.* Publications by trade organizations.

Advertising

- *Standard Directory of Advertising Agencies*

26-2. Interview graduates

Interview three people who recently graduated from your school and received jobs in the area in which you are interested. Ask them what their experiences were – good and bad – in their job search. Also ask them how well or poorly prepared they were for their jobs and what advice they have for getting a job or internship.

26-3. Internet job search

You want to find out what jobs are available in your field. Your textbook mentions job searching opportunities available on the Internet and lists some sites in the chapter as well as in the appendix. In addition to the Online Career Center and job opportunities listed in journalism magazines and on-line sites, there are several other employment and career searching sites on the Internet, some specifically geared to college students. Find at least five other sites that offer information about job opportunities. List the name of the sites and the Internet addresses that you find most helpful.

a. _____

b. _____

c. _____

d. _____

e. _____

26-4. Resume forms

Word processing programs such as Microsoft Word and WordPerfect offer good templates for resumes, but they can be difficult to change. You can try using one of these to write your printed resume. Keep it simple because employers often scan resumes into a database. If you use a template, change any font size that is small than 12 point. Some features on the Microsoft templates are only 8 or 10 points and are very hard to read, especially if they are being scanned.

If you have experience, you may list that first. If you are an undergraduate with little or no experience, consider listing your education first. Put your strongest assets first. Don't list any categories of items that you don't have such as honors or other interests. A sample is on the next page.

26-5. Web resumes

If you know how to create Web pages, try creating a one-screen Web home page to your resume. When you put your resume online, don't use a horizontal format. Web users read from top to bottom. Use a simple format with lists. You can check the Web site for this book for some resources on creating Web pages. You can also save a Word document as an html document – a printer version of a Web document.

Here is a resume adapted from a template in Microsoft Word.

Your Name
E-mail address

School address (if different from home address)   **Home address**
Street   Street
City, state, ZIP   City, State ZIP
Phone   Phone

Objective

To get a job or internship (font size increased to 12 point)

Experience

Years   Name of organization and school
Campus news reporter
Covered features and student government
Created Web site

Summer Year   Internship   Daily Planet News, All city, all state
Reporter
Covered high school sports, wrote news features.

Dates (years)   College Bar and Grill   City, State
Server

Education

Dates (years)   Your State University   Your town, state

Journalism and Mass Communications - Expected graduation date

References

Add another category about honors and awards if you have them or special skills. Also list your URL for a Web site if you have one.

Honors/awards

List three references, phone numbers and e-mail.

161

Appendix - Style Tests

The style tests in this section are designed to give you practice learning some basics of style from the Associated Press Stylebook. The tests are based on style concepts that are frequently used in media writing and some common mistakes. Your instructor may prefer that you study more items than are listed in this study guide. Interactive self-graded quizzes are on the textbook's Web site at *http://info.wadsworth.com/rich*.

A

abbreviations:
  a.m., p.m.,
  addresses
academic degrees
  (bachelor's
  degree, master's
  degree, Ph.D.)
accommodate
addresses (how to
  write them)
affect/effect
ages
aid, aide
allege
all right
alumnus, alumni,
  alumna, alumnae
Alzheimer's
  disease
among/between

B

bachelor's degree
bad/badly
bail
bimonthly

burglary, larceny, robbery, theft
bus, buses

C

cannot
capitalization of titles
capitol
CD-ROM
Centers for Disease Control
cents
civil case/criminal case
City Hall (when to capitalize)
collective nouns
complement, compliment
compose, comprise
congress
congressional
consensus
constitution
couple
court names
criterion, criteria

D

database
days of the week
dean's list
dependent

directions (east,
  west, etc. -when
  to capitalize)
disabled,
  handicapped
distances
doctor
dollars
doughnut
drunk/drunken
Dumpster

E
each
election returns
e-mail
embarrass
employee
espresso
essential/nonessent
  ial clauses
exaggerate

F
federal
felony,
  misdemeanor
fewer/less
flier/flyer

G
good/well
governmental
  bodies

H
harass/harassment
homicide/murder/
  manslaughter
House of
  Representatives

I
Internet
it's/its

J
Jell-O
judge
judgment/judgmental

K
kidnapped
kids
kindergarten
Ku Klux Klan

L
lay/lie
legislature
like/as

M
magazine names
marijuana
Mass (celebrated, not said)
master's degree
media (plural)
mile/when to use figures
mph
millions/billions
months (when to abbreviate)

N
No. 1
none
no one

O
occur, occurred, occurring
OK
online
over/more than

P

passers-by
percentages
plurals
police department
possessives
potato
pounds (spell out
  with figures)
principal/principle
privilege/privileged

Q

quotations in the
  news
quotation
  punctuation

R

religious titles
road (don't
  abbreviate)
Roman Catholic
  Church

S

Senate
sheriff
stationary/stationery
subjunctive mood
Supreme Court

T

teen-ager
temperatures
that/which/who/whom
their/there/they're
time element
titles
totaled
trademark
traveled

U

U.S. Postal Service
U.S. Supreme Court

V

versus
vice versa

W

weather terms (hurricane, blizzard,
  tornado)
Web
White House
who/whom
who's/whose
World Wide Web

X, Y, Z

Xerox
yesterday
zeros
ZIP code (capitalize ZIP)

Style Test A-B

Circle the correct item between parentheses.

1. The conference will be at (10 A.M.   10 a.m.)

2. It is not (alright all right) if you come to class late.

3. I will try to (accomodate accommodate) you if you have a learning

disability.

4. The extra money from fees will be divided (between among) the journalism

department, the Student Senate and the university technology committee.

5. The boy was only (five 5) years old when he learned algebra.

6. Your style tests will (affect effect) your grade.

7. She lives at (2600 Barker Avenue 2600 Barker Ave.)

8. The accident occurred on (Tudor Rd. Tudor Road).

9. She felt (bad badly) about missing class.

10. She is an (alumnus, alumna) of Radcliffe College.

11. Are you getting a (bachelors degree bachelor's degree)?

12. Scientists are seeking a cure for (Alzheimers disease Alzheimer's disease).

13. He was an (aid aide) to the Republican senator from his state.

14. The parade is held every year on (Broad St. Broad Street).

15. The journalism building is at (333 Sunset Rd. 333 Sunset Road).

16. The woman who was injured was (19 years old 19-years-old).

17. She earned her (Ph.D. PH.D.) at the University of Missouri.

18. The intruder threatened the homeowner with a gun while committing a

(robbery, burglary).

19. The public (busses buses) run every hour between the school and

downtown.

20. A (9-year-old, nine-year-old, 9 year old) boy won the spelling bee.

165

Style Test C-E

Circle the correct usage or style.

1. I (cannot, can not) excuse you from class next week.

2. Each of the students (has, have) (his or her, their) own ideas of how to write a good story.

3. Do you enjoy drinking (expresso, espresso) with a (donut, doughnut)?

4. She hasn't been to New York in 20 years, but she still has an (East Coast, east coast) accent.

5. An (employee, employe) at a newspaper needs a respect for deadlines.

6. The journalism department, (which, that) is in Building K, offers good courses.

7. The Board of Regents reached a (consensus, consensus of opinion) to increase tuition rates.

8. The Board of Regents (is, are) meeting again next week to discuss the rates.

9. Martin Luther King Jr.'s birthday was celebrated on (Jan. 18, January 18).

10. If you want to find his house, you have to go (east, East) on (Main Street, Main St.) for (two, 2) miles after you cross Pine Road.

11. The latest information about AIDS is on the Web site for the (Center for Disease Control, Centers for Disease Control).

12. The textbook costs ($37, 37 dollars).

13. He was convicted of (drunk, drunken) driving.

14. These are the students (that, who, which) won scholarships.

15. Introduction to Media Writing is the course (that, which) is required of all journalism majors.

16. Do you use (E-mail, e-mail) frequently?

17. The First Amendment to the (constitution, Constitution) protects freedom of speech.

18. The postal rate was (34 cents, 34¢) for a stamp at the start of the millennium.

19. Some Alaska lawmakers want to move the (capital, capitol) from Juneau to Anchorage.

20. She made the (dean's list, Dean's List) every semester.

166

Style Test F-K

Circle the correct usage or style.

1. Disturbing the peace is usually a (felony, misdemeanor) considered a minor offense with a sentence of less than a year in jail.

2. (Fewer, Less) than 10 students applied for the journalism scholarships offered by the department.

3. They did (good, well) on their style tests.

4. The (U.S. Department of Justice, U.S. department of justice) compiles crime statistics.

5. Sexual (harassment, harrassment) is a crime.

6. The (house of representatives, House of Representatives) voted to impeach the president.

7. This book has a Web site with links to the (internet, Internet).

8. The child's favorite dessert was (jello, Jell-O).

9. The (5-year-old, five-year-old) boy was (kidnapped, kidnaped) after his (kindergarten, kindergarden) class.

10. (Its, It's) a sign of ignorance if you can't tell the difference between these two words.

11. The (Klu Klux Klan, Ku Klux Klan) was planning a march.

12. When you craft a lead, you must use your (judgment, judgement) about what is most important.

13. The students distributed (fliers, flyers) about the public relations meeting.

14. She got (less, fewer) than three items correct on the test.

15. (Kidnapping, kidnaping) is a (federal, Federal) crime.

16. Almost every major city has a beautiful (City Hall, city hall).

17. The woman who killed the driver in the automobile accident was convicted of (murder, manslaughter).

18. How many (kids, children) are in that grade school?

19. My dog loves to chase (its, it's) tail.

20. The meeting will be conducted in Philadelphia (City Hall, city hall).

Style Test L-O

Circle the correct usage or style.

1. Did you (lay, laid, lie) your paper on my desk?

2. She was tired so she (lay, laid, lied) down for a nap.

3. The (legislature, Legislature) in each state includes a house of

representatives and a senate.

4. He behaved (like, as) a child when he could not get his way.

5. A hurricane has winds exceeding 74 (miles per hour, mph).

6. Bill Gates is worth more than ($50 billion, fifty billion dollars, 50 billion

dollars).

7. The city council passed a ($20-million, $20 million) budget.

8. The media (was, were) blamed for poor coverage of the scandal.

9. Three students were charged with selling (marihuana, marijuana).

10. The priest will (say, celebrate) (Mass, mass) this Sunday.

11. The accident (occurred, occured) late last night.

12. The park is (5 miles, five miles) to the east, but the camping grounds are

still (12 miles, twelve miles) from the park entrance.

13. None of the students (was, were) qualified for the job.

14. Millions of people read their news (on-line, online) every day.

15. She earned (over, more than) $50 in tips last week.

16. It is (OK, okay) to bring your friend to class.

17. The football team prided itself on being (Number 1, No. 1) in its league.

18. Do you read ("Time" magazine, Time magazine)?

19. Are you planning to get a (masters degree, master's degree) in journalism?

20. (No one, Noone) in this class is eligible for a tuition waiver.

Style Test P-S

Circle the correct usage or style.

1. If you get (5 percent, 5%, five percent) of these sentences wrong, you will have a grade of (95 percent, 95%).

2. Several officers in the Los Angeles (Police Department, police department) were fired.

3. How many (potatoes, potatos) are in a bushel?

4. She weighs (125 lbs., 125 pounds).

5. The accident occurred at (233 Mountain Rd., 233 Mountain Road).

6. "I am (innocent," innocent",) the suspect said.

7. Do not use your office (stationery, stationary) for personal correspondence.

8. The (sheriff, sherrif) is an elected officer.

9. The (supreme court, Supreme Court) ruled that Internet service providers are not responsible for libelous information posted by people who use their service.

10. If she (was, were) planning to major in journalism, she would have enrolled in the program by now.

11. Several (passer-bys, passers-by, passersby) saw the accident.

12. The (principal, principle) behind the First Amendment is to protect people's right to express themselves in a democracy.

13. (The Rev. John Paul, Father John Paul) is the priest in this parish.

14. If I (was, were) in your position, I would have complained to the professor.

15. The choices for you are enclosed in (parenthesis, parentheses).

16. Internet usage soared during the (1990's, 1990s).

17. She had all (As, A's) on her transcript.

18. Many speakers start their speeches by saying they are (priveleged, privileged, priviledged) to be here.

19. Martin Luther King Jr. said, ("We shall overcome." "We shall overcome".)

20. The (Senate, senate) conducted the impeachment trial of the president.

Style Test T-Z

Circle the correct usage or style.

1. The (teenager, teen-ager) admitted stealing the candy.

2. The personnel director, (that, who, which) reviews the applications, is on vacation.

3. This book has a site on the (world wide web, World Wide Web).

4. The building (that, which) houses the administration is on Adams Street.

5. The professor (who's, whose) tests were stolen is in the English department.

6. (Who, Whom) were you going to contact about the job?

7. Make sure you include your (zip, Zip, ZIP) code when you send your resume.

8. A snowstorm must have winds of (35 mph, 75 mph) or more to be considered a blizzard.

9. The game, Duke (versus, vs.) University of North Carolina, is sold out.

10. A tornado (warning, watch) alerts the public of an existing tornado in the area.

11. Did you make a copy on the (Xerox, xerox) machine?

12. (Who's Whose) going to be class president?

13. Did you send the package by Federal Express or the (postal service, Postal Service)?

14. My friends wanted to join me, but I don't know if (their, they're, there) going to be at the game.

15. When the server (totalled, totaled) the bill, it came to $100.

16. The student (traveled, travelled) to Paris last summer.

17. Do you have a (web, Web) page?

18. Do you know (who, whom) is to blame for this mess?

19. This is the woman (who, whom) I asked you to contact.

20. Former (Sen. Senator) John Glenn was 77 years old when he traveled into space aboard the shuttle Discovery.